THE KNOWLEDGE
OF MAN

THE KNOWLEDGE OF MAN

Selected Essays

MARTIN BUBER

EDITED WITH AN INTRODUCTORY ESSAY BY
Maurice Friedman

TRANSLATED BY
MAURICE FRIEDMAN AND RONALD GREGOR SMITH
NEW INTRODUCTION BY
Alan Udoff
Baltimore Hebrew University

HUMANITIES PRESS INTERNATIONAL, INC.
ATLANTIC HIGHLANDS, NJ

This edition first published with a new introduction 1988 in the United
States of America by Humanities Press International, Inc., Atlantic
Highlands, NJ 07716

Reprinted 1989, 1991, 1992

Library of Congress Cataloging-in-Publication Data

Buber, Martin, 1878–1964.
　　[Selections. English. 1988]
　　The knowledge of man : selected essays / Martin Buber ; edited
with an introductory essay by Maurice Friedman ; translated by
Maurice Friedman and Ronald Gregor Smith ; new introduction
by Alan Udoff.
　　　　p.　　cm.
　　Reprint. Originally published: London : Allen & Unwin, 1965.
　　Includes index.
　　ISBN 0–391–03546–0 (pbk.)
　　1. Philosophical anthropology.　2. Interpersonal relations—
Philosophy.　I. Friedman, Maurice S.　II. Title.
B3213.B82E52 1988
128—dc19　　　　　　　　　　　　　　　　　　　　　　88–12825
　　　　　　　　　　　　　　　　　　　　　　　　　　　　　　　CIP

Printed in the United States of America

CONTENTS

EDITOR'S FOREWORD

It has been eleven years since Martin Buber and I met with the Religious Book department of Harper's to discuss the plans for Professor Buber's forthcoming philosophical anthropology: his study of the problem of man. Because of his great work translating the Hebrew Bible into German and because of the thousand other demands on his time, Professor Buber told me then that it would be a matter of grace if he were allowed to finish his anthropology. This grace was given him. Martin Buber is the most impressive example I know of what he himself wrote about a friend in his book *Eclipse of God*: 'To be old is a glorious thing when one has not unlearned what it means to *begin*.' Martin Buber is 'old in a young way, knowing how to begin'. His philosophical anthropology represents an exciting new beginning in his thought—begun at the age of seventy-three and completed just after his eighty-fifth birthday!

Martin Buber's philosophical anthropology has been a special concern of mine—in the Quaker sense of the term. Because of this concern I have gone beyond the boundaries that are customary for an editor and I have added as the first chapter of this book an 'Introductory Essay' of my own. Its thirteen sections serve to set Buber's essays on 'the knowledge of man' in the context of his philosophy of dialogue as well as to show their interrelations and their significance for other fields of thought. Martin Buber has himself gone over this 'Introductory Essay' (of which he writes me, 'Probably it is the best you have written on my thought') and has made suggestions for clarification of several passages that he found unclear.

Professor Buber has also read carefully all the translations from the German, and in many cases the final form is the product of a number of interchanges between us as to what word or words would best express his thought. 'Distance and Relation' and 'Elements of the Interhuman' were translated by Ronald Gregor Smith, Professor of Theology at the University of Glasgow and translator of Buber's classic works *I and Thou* and *Between Man and Man*. The translation of 'Elements of the Interhuman' was thoroughly revised by Professor Buber and myself before its publication in *Psychiatry* in 1957. 'What Is Common to All', 'The Word That Is Spoken', 'Guilt and Guilt Feelings', and 'Man and His Image-Work' were all translated by me.

'Distance and Relation' was originally published in the *Hibbert Journal*, Vol. XLIX (1951), and was reprinted along with 'Elements of the Interhuman' and 'Guilt and Guilt Feelings' in *Psychiatry*, Vol. XX, No. 2 (May 1957) as the William Alanson White Memorial Lectures, Fourth Series. These lectures were given in Washington, D.C., in the spring of 1957 under the sponsorship of the Washington School of Psychiatry, which brought Martin Buber to America. It was in particular the iniative of Dr Leslie H. Farber, then Chairman of the Faculty of the Washington School of Psychiatry, that made both this lecture series and the seminars on the unconscious, which I summarize in Section 8 of my 'Introductory Essay', a reality. 'What Is Common to All' was published in the *Review of Metaphysics*, Vol. XI, No. 3 (March 1958). 'The Word That Is Spoken' was published in *Modern Age*, Vol. V, No. 4 (Fall 1961). 'Man and His Image-Work' was published in *Portfolio*, Vol. VII (Winter 1963). All of these essays are copyrighted by Martin Buber. Professor Buber has agreed to my suggestion of including as an appendix to this book the dialogue between Carl R. Rogers and him that I moderated at the University of Michigan in April 1957. It brings out important implications of Buber's thought that have not been written elsewhere. This dialogue was published in *Psychologia—An International Journal of Psychology in the Orient*, Vol III, No. 4 (Kyoto University, December 1960) and is reprinted with the permission of its editor and of Dr Carl R. Rogers, Professor of Psychology and Psychiatry at the University of Wisconsin.

The original of all Buber's essays in *The Knowledge of Man* may be found in Martin Buber, *Werke*, Vol. I, *Schriften zur Philosophie* (Munich and Heidelberg: Kösel Verlag and Verlag Lambert Schneider, 1962), pp. 267–290, 411–502.

MAURICE FRIEDMAN

Bronxville, New York   *Professor of Philosophy*
March 1963   *Sarah Lawrence College*

INTRODUCTION

We are condemned to philosophize "between tradition and
another beginning." The reference here to "another beginning" indicates an "otherness" or "new way of experiencing
and thinking" towards which our age strives. I refer, for
example, to the thought of Rosenzweig, Buber, Jaspers,
Sartre, Marcel, Maritain, and above all Heidegger.

In this *Postscript* to his "Hermeneutics and the History of Being,"[1]
Werner Marx repeats, with certain variations, the divided line of the
"new thinking" that Karl Löwith had drawn in "M. Heidegger and
F. Rosenzweig: A Postscript to *Being and Time.*"[2] Löwith's division
traces two lines of genealogical descent: from the dialogism of
Feuerbach and the existentialism of Kierkegaard. The former has
among its principal representatives Ebner, Ehrenberg, Buber, and
Rosenstock; the latter, Barth, Gogarten, Jaspers, Grisebach, and
Heidegger. Overarching the differences that distinguish these representatives, whose exemplars include Cohen and Rosenzweig, is a
common horizon or "spirit of the age." With Heidegger and Rosenzweig as his referents, Löwith defines that horizon in this way:

> Each man directed his thought away from the metaphysic of
> consciousness of German idealism while at the same time each
> one avoided positivism. Positively viewed, each took the "fac-
> ticity" of human *Dasein* as his common starting point.[3]

That is to say, each man constituted both an end and a beginning.
    The intention of the following introductory remarks is to situate
Buber over against this horizon of end and beginning, to themati-
cally re-originate the question of his place in the radical spirit of a
revolutionary age that shares the destiny of "every brute inversion
of the world . . . that knows the disinherited to whom the past no
longer belongs, and not yet the future."[4] To this end, the texts of

Marx and Löwith contribute in a double capacity—not only in the content of their judgment, but in the form or genre of its pronouncement. For it is the genre of the *postscript*, or more exactly, the trace or presentiment that repeats itself within that genre, that fatefully names what is at issue and at stake in the inquiry at hand. It is as if these scholarly *postscripts*, in reflecting upon the thinking of this age, bear uncannily the trace of that age's most radical thought— the thought that, in perceiving itself as end and beginning, self-consciously expresses itself *in* and *as* a writing-that-comes-after-the-end-of-writing-that-is-philosophy. The remarks that follow are intended, then, to clear one path along which thinking as post-scription may move in an encounter with Buber and his texts.[5] The direction, if not the actual means of this clearing, is already available in Emmanuel Levinas's "Martin Buber, Gabriel Marcel, and Philosophy"[6]—indeed, in the very title, where the conjunction *and*, as in so many of Levinas's works, gestures toward a path of engagement rather than the mere reflex of academic comparisons.

To summarize the salient points of Levinas's account: "According to the letter of the texts" in which Buber breaks with subject-object ontology—the very texts in which he privileges the vehicles of that break: the *encounter*, the *relationship*, the *between*—the call of being, defined as presence or co-presence, itself breaks through as "the ultimate support of meaning." [307] The call comes as the recuperative address to "rejoin the lofty Western tradition for which . . . every relationship with being is, in the final analysis, reducible to an experience (that is, to a knowledge) and remains a modality of that being." [308] It is this call of the "vocation of philosophy" to which dialogical thinking must "respond." [313]

"What was that vocation?"[7] In its "negative definition," the unwillingness to "submit passively" to the *doxa* of the city, to "ideologies"; "in the final analysis, it is to be able to say *I*, to think while saying *I*, to be able to say in all sincerity: *cogito*."[8] Positively, "what assured that power . . . was objective knowledge," whose "rigorous development . . . led, indeed, to the full consciousness of self. To think being is to think to its measure and to coincide with oneself." It is against the vocation of philosophy thus conceived, and within the "growing uncertainty as to the exact extent of the domain of thought won from opinion and ideology" [313]—an uncertainty that has climaxed in the " 'merciless critical search' " of contemporary French philosophy's critique of the "privilege of presence" [314]—that the question of Buber (and Marcel) is raised:

> . . . does their contestation of the philosophical privilege of the *relationship* to the *Other* understood as a *being* thematised and assimilable to knowledge by virtue of the ideal generalities, their doctrine of the *relationship to the Other* assuring the otherness of the Other and thus his transcendence, as that of a Thou addressed in God and in the other man encountered in the wake of that address—does that thought respond to the vocation of philosophy? [314]

At the reading surface of Levinas's text, a direct answer may be found:

> The I-Thou relationship, the reciprocity of dialogue, which sustains all human conversation, is described in Buber as a pure and in some sense formal face-to-face confrontation, but then appears immediately as qualified: responsibility of the one for the other, as if the "face to face" were from the start, and always, an ethical concreteness. . . . Buber's entire *oeuvre* is a renewal of ethics. . . . An ethic of heteronomy which is not a servitude. . . .
>
> But this new ethic is also a new way of understanding the possibility of an I, and therefore it responds to the vocation of philosophy.
>
> This is an ethical interpretation of transcendence, but it is certainly not always preserved from falling back into a vision in which the I-Thou—the ethical—is interpreted once again as a certain—priviledged—mode of presence, that is as a modality of being.
>
> The interpretation of the I-Thou relationship as presence, . . . [does it not] in the final analysis, attest to the impossibility of thinking outside being or beyond being? In that case dialogic philosophy would merely be a specification of ontology and the 'thought' . . . in the Heideggerian sense, or transcendental idealism. [317–318]

There is, however, another sur*face* along which the direction of (this) reading moves.

In contrast to Marcel's derivation of "the I-Thou from a previous, deeper bond which is not dialogic—from the structure of incarnation and ontological mystery," Buber situates the ultimacy and irreducibility of the I-Thou within the dialogic of language; within "the what-is-said of Saying as such"; the "Saying that says Thou", the singular case of addressivity—i.e., "the incomparable *case* among the other *cases* of the declension": the vocative that stands over against the call of the vocation of philosophy. [315–316] It is in "the pure allegiance and responsibility" of this dialogic, a responsibility which "precedes all knowledge," that Levinas *interpretively* locates Buber *and himself* with reference to the vocation of philosophy [316]: that is to say, through a radical transcendentalization of the ethical, Levinas—"taking a few steps to one side of Buber"—moves to "rejoin" him.[9] [316]

In effect, Levinas's reading of Buber constitutes an e-vocation of his texts; of the vocative in which they are grounded; a call to the call of his texts; a response that is a rejoining—not simply a rejoinder; an "allegiance to the Other" [318] of the text, in whose texture the "persistence of ontology" [307] resonates, and to which the vocation of philosophy itself *thereby* responds—calling *it* to "rejoin the lofty Western tradition of Being." [308] It is against this invocation, against "the destiny of philosophy which has been transmitted to us" [318] that Levinas clears a path, through a dialogical reading, to, or for, the question of Buber. This question, then, if asked *rightly*, includes the question of meeting within the space of reading. Not metaphorically, but actually. Insofar as the genre of *introduction* defines itself with reference to this actuality, it must, particularly in the case of Buber, position itself mediately between the internal dialogue of text and sub-text, as well as the externality of text and context. Within the economy of this genre, it is only possible to demarcate along the path of reading the theoretical borderline of these mediations.

Levinas's *way* of reading—"it is by identifying the subtextual language of particular discourses that we can decide whether they are philosophical or not"[10]—places us on the path of Buber's texts. These texts are, by Buber's own account, philosophical. In a sense, then, they may be thought of as belonging to the vocation of philosophy. However, the nature of that belonging or participation proves problematical as soon as one enters upon the course of that account.[11] In accord with the nuances of the latter, it is necessary then to turn, albeit selectively, to the texts themselves:

> The real stream of thinking . . . [includes] a noetic movement from a personal meeting to a factual knowledge-structure, a movement in which the two primal words cooperate, as it were. Authentic philosophizing orginates ever anew from the fulgurations of the Thou relationship that still affords no "objective" knowledge. Now the transposition into the structured order of It takes place, and, if a real workman is at work, there may stand at the end the freestone structure of a system. Indeed, "I-It finds its highest [sic] concentration and clarification in philosophical knowledge": but that in no way means that this knowledge contains nothing other than I-It, is nothing other than I-It. The fiery track of the original fulgurations is inextinguishable, even though it may remain unnoticed by the eye accustomed to an objectified image of being. To the penetrating genesis-glance each bold metaphysical setting manifests its origin in a meeting of the knowing person with an element of being that announces itself in the shape of that which meets him in a living way.[12]

This passage, as it were, sets a seal on the question at hand. At the same time it suggests the line along which that seal may be opened and the question of Buber and the vocation of philosophy raised anew.

The binary opposition that structures and encodes Buber's thought—the primal words or domains of the I-Thou/I-It—is repeated here in the depiction of thinking itself: the "real stream of thinking" that moves between the privileged plenitude of relationship and origin, and the opposing border of philosophical knowledge in which the I-It achieves its apotheosis. For Buber, the history of the spirit is, in one critically important sense, the growing hegemony of the latter which, standing as "the freestone structure of a system," casts its shadow over its ownmost origins as thinking—over the I-Thou, over the space of meeting and the "living way."[13]

In the chiaroscuro of this history, the history of the spirit as the alternation of light and darkness, the history which culminates in light as alternation,[14] the eye is seen as the singular, metonymic point of reference:

> Contemplation, the visual, optic life, means recourse to ideal notions. Knowledge of the object, impossible without idealization, is merely the freezing of an existential state. It puts an end to the personal plenitude achieved in the encounter, in relationship, in the covenant between single ones, which rests solely on the pure co-existence of the I with the absolute Thou, on the *with* which is pure transcendence.[15] [308]

It is against the pan*oramic* horizon which philosophy claims as its preserve, which assimilates the face of particularity into the "objectified image of being," that Buber's concluding statements must be positioned. Buber's re-view of the course of thinking is turned toward the plenitude of meeting as a recoverable trace within the philosophical horizon. The axis of that recovery turns on the "genesis-glance," on seeing as a *recuperative* act.[16] Through this seeing, the *thou* of the other—in the manifold expressions that alterity assumes—may be authentically en-visioned. It is precisely this form of seeing that Buber opposes to the philosophical vision: "the eye accustomed to an objectified image of being." The scene of this opposition may encompass every manifestation of alterity—although the actuality of the engagement depends ultimately on the fortuitous conjunction of will and grace. The case at hand is exemplary.

"Every essential knowledge," Buber's text continues, "is in its origin contact with an existing being and in its completion possession of an enduring concept." The re-origination of that contact, the trajectory of the movement of the recuperation of encounter, may be conceived along the lines—literally so—of a re-tracing; i.e., a re-covering-through-the-trace (through the "fiery track of the original fulgurations") of the plenitude of presence. This recovery cannot be *event*ualized through an act of re-conceptualization: "The concrete, from which all philosophizing starts, cannot again be reached by way of philosophical abstraction; it is suspended [*aufgehoben*]."[17] Rather, it may only be pointed to; with the "thinking, the teaching . . . determined by the task of pointing."[18]

These qualifications apply equally to the text as the scene of opposition—where seeing is an act of recuperative reading, a hermeneutical en-visioning—where hermeneutics "is understood as the manifestation and restoration of a meaning addressed to me in the manner of a message, a proclamation, . . . a kerygma."[19] In the instance of Buber's texts, the qualifications may be applied, in part, in the following way: Buber's writings, particularly in which the works of others are to be dialogically engaged, would recuperatively preserve against the instrumentality of their own analytical texts the sub-textual trace of their origin as meeting. That is, Buber's writings, often through tactical tropes and word plays, or strategies of rhythm, repetition, and cititation (the list is not exhaustive) point to the eventuations and the alternations of meeting and distance that they would strive to achieve, on the one hand, and yet necessarily submit to, on the other.

With these qualifications in mind, the question, "How does dialogue respond to the essential vocation of philosophy?"—the question that Levinas asks enroute to the endpoint of "alternation"—must be extended to include the relation of the dialogical text to the vocation of philosophy, where the text itself would be marked by the alternation of the primal realms of meeting and distance that it describes; the text that, in its very alternations, would fatefully attest to the "sacrifice and risk" at back of its creation;[20] the text that "is doomed by its nature to become a thing or at least to enter into thinghood again and again."[21] The dialogical text as work recalls, thereby, the work of art, with this fundamental difference: in contrast to "the eternal origin of art," where "a human being confronts a form that wants to become a work through him,"[22] philosophy is the perennial form that this fatefulness takes when "man lifts himself above the concrete situation into the sphere of precise conceptualization."[23] In recalling the reason for his own submission to this fatefulness, Buber reveals something of the nature of the writings that ensued:

> I have stood under the duty to insert the framework of the decisive experiences that I had . . . into the human inheritance of thought, but not as 'my' experiences, rather as an insight valid and important for others and even for other kinds of men. Since, however, I have received no message which might

be passed on in such a manner, but have only had the experiences and attained the insights, my communication had to be a philosophical one. It had to relate the unique and particular to the "general." . . . It had to express what is by its nature incomprehensible in concepts that could be used and communicated. . . . More precisely, I had to make an It out of that which was experienced in I-Thou and as I-Thou.[24]

In what sense, then, do these writings "respond to the essential vocation of philosophy"? In a profoundly suggestive way, philosophy is depicted here as arising *in want*—not in the erotic sense of the Platonic *between*, but *in want of the between* that consists in the plenitude of the primal realm of I-Thou, in the fullness of meeting. Buber's own *need* for philosophy, for "the indispensable logicizing of reality,"[25] results from the desire to point to that fullness: "[To] bear witness to an experience"; "showing that experience to be one accessible to all men in some measure, in some form."[26] Out of this desire, which, by the nature of desire binds, Buber experiences the need for philosophy:

> I am not merely bound to philosophical language. I am bound to the philosophical method, indeed to a dialectic that has become unavoidable with the beginning of philosophical thinking. . . . My philosophy serves . . . an experienced, a perceived attitude that it has been established to make communicable.[27]

In serving the end of this desire, Buber's writings necessarily enter the path of the history of philosophy, or the record of its "essential vocation." It must not be assumed, however, that the history and vocation of philosophy are identical; or, if such an identity does obtain, that the meaning of the vocation of philosophy has not long since been falsified in the course of that history. Indeed, Buber's own observation of his place on this path—"I do not feel myself far . . . from the Platonic dialogues"[28] is instructive to this end. That is, Buber's failure to perceive the distance that separates him from the *Dialogues* may be attributed to the more fundamental failure to grasp the way in which the *Dialogues* conceive of the origin and radicality of philosophy. The consequences of this failure reach to the very endpoint of the question that frames all that has preceded: the way in which Buber's thought may be said to "respond to the essential vocation of philosophy."

For Buber, the response turns on the recuperative reappropriation of philosophy. As the object of this recuperation, philosophy is designated the ultimate instrument of conceptual analysis—where analysis itself is accorded the penultimate role of "gateway"; i.e., the necessary way to a goal that "itself cannot be grasped philosophically."[29] Herein lies both the limit of philosophy's domain and the source of its commanding governance; for philosophy's achievement, and whatever degree of ultimacy may be ascribed to it, derives from the fact that "it radically abandoned the relation with the concrete"[30] while, at the same time, providing the concepts and categories for "a full comprehension and presentation" of its transmissible structure.[31] Thus, whereas the primal realm of the I-Thou is constituted by the meeting of will and grace, the "objective thought-continuum" in which philosophy culminates requires no such conjunction: "Every man who can 'think' may enter this continuum through the simple use of this ability, through a thinking comprehension of thought."[32]

The path toward the question of the "essential vocation of philosophy" has itself thus come to rest on a path, or "continuum," whose entry point is "thinking" and whose exit lies under the sign of thinking's *want* of completion: the "gateway" that points beyond. Insofar as that path consists in writing, insofar as it has come to rest in a text, it too must point beyond. The limit that Buber *ascribes* to philosophy will have to literalize itself; not in the form of an *after*thought or *post*script, an appendix to the body of the work. Rather, the work, as thought and text, will have to recuperatively embody, or point to, or trace that which lies beyond even as it appears in the attenuation of its presence. That is to say, the text will have to take the form of a kind of post-scription: a writing-that-comes-after-the-writing-that-is-philosophy. It is this form of post-scription that Buber designates "conversation,"[33] and it is by this designation that he would understand his own efforts.[34]

With these texts and observations in place it is possible to offer, by way of conclusion, the texts and observations that follow.

The most fundamental level at which Buber may be read is on the ground of the difference of I-Thou and I-It. To read Buber in this way is to read him ultimately in light of the difference between the dialogical and the philosophical, within the horizon of the question: "How does dialogue respond to the essential vocation of philosophy?" This question in the end, stands or falls on the understanding of philosophy, or the path along which it moves. As understood by Buber, the path of philosophy is not essentially different from the course of its history—or, one might say, its doxography. On the basis of this understanding, the recovery of the I-Thou from the traces of its dispersal in the I-It, i.e., the recuperation of philosophy, will not take the form of the overcoming of the history of philosophy, the carrying it through to its destruction, but, rather, of the overcoming of philosophy as such. The movement of this recuperation begins with philosophy's own beginning in the opening of thinking as "the primary act of abstraction,"[35] and ends with its closure at the point or moment at which thinking becomes a "gateway" to that which is irrecoverable by thinking itself: the concrete situation.

Buber's account of this beginning reads:

> Philosophizing and philosophy . . . begin ever anew with one's definitely looking away from his concrete situation, hence with the primary act of abstraction.
>
> What is meant here by abstraction is simple, anthropological matter of fact and not the 'radical' abstraction with which Hegel demands that the philosopher begin.[36]

What is to be noted in this account is the way in which the optics of philosophy have been reduced to the focal aggression of a "looking away from," in place of the seeing-as-wonder by which, for example, Plato and Aristotle described the originary arc of philosophy's vision. That is, Buber situates in the "concrete reality from which the philosophizing man does and must look away"[37] the plenitude that wonder in its radicality *as* philosophy dis-covers. Buber thus aligns himself with the modern view that re-originates philosophy's origin in the aggression of doubt, calculation, and mastery, as opposed to the openness to Being, that classically defines it.[38] The reference to Hegel, moreover, underscores what is at stake in Buber's account; for it is precisely the critical distinctions that Hegel introduces in the preface to *The Phenomenology of Spirit* between the "natural consciousness" of ancient times and its modern counterpart, in which "the individual finds the abstract form ready made," that argue decisively against any conception of abstraction as a "simple, anthropological matter of fact," or any conception of philosophy that itself does not distinguish between philosophizing as an act of differentiation and as an act of concretization. Were the implications of these distinctions followed to their endpoint, one would find, as well, the reason why Buber may speak of philosophy's tendency to "begin ever anew," that is, the reason why the very presence of philosophy is not for Buber intrinsically problematical.

However the notion of philosophy's *beginning ever anew* is determined, it remains for Buber a repetition within the domain of the I-It, within regional boundaries defined by a "looking away from," and the "gateway" that opens into return. That to which the return is made—what Buber has denominated (for here description has already begun to pass into address) "*one* great experience of faith"—can only be indicated (in the strict etymological sense of pointing):

> By this is meant an experience that transports a person in all his component parts, his capacity for thought certainly included, so that, all the doors springing open, the storm blows through all the chambers.[39]

To speak of the inclusion of thought in this experience of faith is to raise, in yet another formulation, the abiding question of the response of dialogue to the "essential vocation of philosophy." It is, thereby, yet another formulation of the question of post-scription or, more generally, boundary.

The metaphor of boundary is coterminous with the more frequent expressions of movement that comprise the inflection and idiom of Buber's discourse. The movement of philosophy, or "the philosophical attitude," is in essence "the product of a consciousness which conceives of itself as autonomous and strives to become so."[40] What is implied in this reference to "autonomy," what Buber describes elsewhere as "reason . . . in its detached autocratic form,"[41] is rendered most exactly in the contrast between religious reality (where the *I-Thou finds its highest intensification and clarification*) and philosophical knowledge" (where the I-It finds its highest intensification and clarification):[42]

> In religious reality the person has concentrated himself into a whole, for it is only as a unified being that he is able to live religiously. In this wholeness thought is naturally also included as an autonomous province but one which no longer strives to absolutize its autonomy. A totalization also takes place in genuine philosophers but no unification. Instead, thinking overruns [*überzieht*] and overwhelms [*überwältigt*] all the faculties and provinces of the person.[43]

The multiple paths of comments and interrogation opened by this text, for the present, must remain unexplored. In their place, the direction of a single question may be pursued to a conclusion. That to which Buber points by the de*sign*ation "overrun" consists not merely in the notion of movement, but this notion raised metaphorically to the level of fatefulness that separates the primal realms of being *and* meaning. That fatefulness, as Levinas observes in reference to Marcel, has as its end not dialogic relationship, but ontologic mystery: Marcel "is concerned with a concrete life which overflows [*qui se déborder*] and leads man to the heart of his being."[44] This totalizing movement appears, in Buber, as the course and dis-course of dialogue:

> In the dialogue between man and man given and received contents are so manifold that he who treats the nature of dialogue as a basic relationship of human existence cannot keep them in mind. Naturally, the contents in general allow generally valid and generally binding propositions to be transmitted; but in so doing the peculiar, that which by its nature is unique, is lost.[45]

The question of the response of dialogue "to the essential vocation of philosophy" may now be reformulated as the question of the boundary of the "overrun"—whether, in Derrida's formulation, "[W]hat has happened, if it has happened, is a sort of overrun [débordement] that spoils all . . . boundaries."[46] The presence of all boundaries; the boundary of Presence. That is to say, the question has become the question of that post-scription which, for want of a better word, is denominated post-modernism.

Alan Udoff

NOTES

1. In *Hermeneutics and Deconstruction*, ed. H. J. Silverman and D. Ihde (Albany: State University of New York Press, 1985), p. 79.
2. In Karl Löwith, *Nature, History, and Existentialism* (Evanston: Northwestern University Press, 1966), pp. 52–53.
3. Ibid., p. 52.
4. *Duino Elegies*. The translation of the verse appears in Walter Kaufmann, *From Shakespeare to Existentialism* (Garden City: Anchor Books, 1960), p. 225. Rilke and Buber stand to each other in a mutually illuminating relationship that embraces Celan as well—and that yet remains to be adequately explored.
5. On the neglected question of the *post*, see Rainer Nägele, *Reading after Freud* (New York: Columbia University Press, 1987).
6. Emmanuel Levinas, "Martin Buber, Gabriel Marcel, and Philosophy," *Martin Buber: A Centenary Volume*, ed. H. Gordon and J. Bloch (New York: KTAV Publishing House, Inc., 1984), pp. 305–321. References to this work are indicated in brackets in the text.
7. Against the understanding of philosophical vocation as work or profession, see Joseph Pieper, *Leisure the Basis of Culture* (New York: Mentor-Omega Books, 1963).
8. It is important to note, if only in passing, what Levinas omits and includes at this point—which begins indiscriminately in a fusion of horizons (opinion/ideology), and ends in the subjectivism of the *cogito*: on the one hand, the courage or, in keeping with the tenor of the passage, resoluteness of philosophy's stand is stripped of its transcendent reference (cf. Plato's *Republic*: 486a–b, and the corresponding commentary of Averroes), on the other, the *cogito* is infused with an ethical transcendence: "to be able to say in all sincerity."
9. See Theodore de Boer, "An Ethical Transcendental Philosophy," in *Face to Face with Levinas*, ed. R. A. Cohen (Albany: State University of New York Press, 1986), pp. 83–115.
10. E. Levinas and R. Kearney, "Dialogue with Emmanuel Levinas," in *Face to Face with Levinas*; pp. 18–19.
11. Irrespective of where Buber is placed in the line of modern philosophical descent—dialogism or existentialism—his relation to philosophy, as such, remains problematical:

"I call my philosophy "dialogical philosophy" not without a certain irony, because basically it cannot be pursued otherwise than dialogically, but the writings dealing with it have been cast into the, for the most part, quite undialogically constituted human world of this hour—and must be cast there.

"Philosophy of existence" appears to me an imprecise and unsteady concept. I have never included myself in such, but feel myself as standing perhaps between an existential thinking in Kierkegaard's sense and something entirely different, something which is still out of sight.

Philosophical Interrogations, ed. S. and B. Rome (New York: Holt, Rinehart and Winston, 1964), p. 23. Cited hereafter as *PI*.

12. Martin Buber, "Replies to My Critics," in *The Philosophy of Martin Buber*, ed. P. A. Schilpp and M. Friedman (La Salle: Open Court Publishing Co., 1967), p. 692. Cited hereafter as "Replies."

13. See *The Eclipse of God*, pp. 123–129. Cited hereafter as *EG*.

14. "Has not the philosophy of dialogue made us attentive to the ambiguity or the enigma of thoughts which link together the world and the other human, knowledge and sociality, being and God? Is not alternation, from now on, the lot of a modern spirit?" E. Levinas [320].

15. As formulated by Buber in *EG* (pp. 40–41):

> The Greeks established the hegemony of the sense of sight over the other senses, thus making the optical world into *the* world. . . . Correspondingly, they also gave to philosophizing, . . . an optical character. . . . The history of Greek philosophy is that of an opticizing of thought. . . . The object of this visual thought is the universal existence or as a reality higher than existence. Philosophy is grounded on the presupposition that one sees the absolute in universals.

16. This "*seeing*" is to be understood actually, not metaphorically:

> Whoever is sent forth in a revelation takes with him in his eyes an image of God; however supra-sensible it may be, he takes it along in the eye of his spirit, in the altogether not metaphorical but entirely real visual power of his spirit.

Martin Buber, *I and Thou*, trans. W. Kaufmann (New York: Charles Scribner's Sons, 1970), p. 166.

17. *EG*, p. 40 (trans. amended).

18. "Replies," p. 693.

19. Paul Ricoeur, *Freud and Philosophy: An Essay on Interpretation*, trans. D. Savage (New Haven: Yale University Press, 1970), p. 27.

20. See *I and Thou*, p. 60.

21. Ibid., p. 69.

22. Ibid., p. 60.

23. Ibid., p. 39.

24. "Replies," p. 689.

25. *PI*, p. 17.

26. *PI*, p. 18.

27. "Replies," pp. 690–691.

28. *PI*, p. 18.

29. *PI*, p. 17. "The concrete, that from which all philosophizing starts, cannot again be reached by way of philosophical abstraction: it is irrevocable." *EG*, p. 40.

30. *EG*, p. 43.

31. *PI*, p. 27.

32. *EG*, p. 43.

33. The status of conversation in Buber's thought differs fundamentally, then, from

its corresponding place in Oakeshott or Rorty. On the latter, cf. Giles Gunn, *The Culture of Criticism and the Criticism of Culture* (New York: Oxford University Press, 1987), pp. 63ff.

34. "Replies," p. 693. Buber's description of those efforts should be carefully noted:

> I had to make an It out of that which was experienced in I-Thou and as I-Thou.
> I am convinced that it happened not otherwise with all the philosopher loved and honored by me. Only that after they had completed the transformation, they devoted themselves to the philosophy more deeply and fully than I was able or it was granted me to do. ("Replies," p. 689.)

It is the body of this difference that the idiom and composition of Buber's texts would incorporate: "No system was suitable for what I had to say. Structure was suitable for it, a compact structure but not one that joined everything together." ("Replies," p. 693.)

35. *EG*, p. 38.
36. Ibid.
37. Ibid., p. 39.
38. It is important to recall in this context the way in which the re-origination of seeing as power, in place of seeing as knowing, is one of the foundation stones of modern philosophy. Thus Descartes begins his *Optics*:

> The conduct of our life depends entirely on our senses, and since sight is the noblest and most comprehensive of the senses, inventions which serve to increase its power are undoubtedly among the most useful there can be.

See *The Philosophical Writings of Descartes*, vol. i, trans. Cottingham, et al. (Cambridge: Cambridge University Press, 1985), p. 152.

39. "Replies," pp. 689–690.
40. *EG*, p. 32.
41. "Replies," p. 690.
42. See *EG*, pp. 44–45.
43. Ibid. p. 44.
44. E. Levinas, [311].
45. "Replies," p. 697.
46. Jacques Derrida, "Living On: Border Lines," in *Deconstruction and Criticism*, ed. G. Hartman (New York: Seabury Press, 1979), p. 70. As a gloss on the final form of the question, cf. Irene E. Harvey, *Derrida and the Economy of Différance* (Bloomington: Indiana University Press, 1986), pp. 169ff.

CHAPTER I

INTRODUCTORY ESSAY

MAURICE FRIEDMAN

1

With this volume Martin Buber completes the last and one of the most significant stages in the development of his philosophical thought, and in particular of his philosophical anthropology, his study of what is peculiar to man as man. Many philosophically minded readers will welcome *The Knowledge of Man* as Buber's most systematic and explicit presentation of his philosophy. These essays represent an important and exciting new development in Buber's philosophy of dialogue; they stand as the culmination and crown of his epistemology, his philosophical anthropology, and his ontology. If we must characterize Buber at all, we can best call him a philosophical anthropologist. In doing so, we do not limit the significance of Buber's philosophy to the human, but we recognize that man's access to being, according to Buber, is not through Plato's ideal forms or Heidegger's being that shines forth in the existent, but through 'the between'—the dialogue between man and the existent over against him.

Although the development of Buber's philosophy of dialogue dates back to the first decade of this century, it reached its maturity and found its classic expression in *I and Thou* (1923). *I and Thou* begins from experience rather than abstract concepts, experience which points to what is the human in man. It is this approach to philosophy that has made Buber's thought a part of that confluence and divergence of streams of thought known as 'existentialism'. At the same time, Buber's existentialism of dialogue brings into sharp focus the radical divergence between the emphasis of thinkers such as Søren Kierkegaard, Martin Heidegger, and Jean-Paul Sartre on the existential subject and the emphasis of thinkers such as Buber, Franz Rosenzweig, and Gabriel Marcel on dialogue, or 'the between'.

2

Man's two primary attitudes and relations, according to *I and Thou*, are 'I–Thou' and 'I–It'. The I of man comes into being in the act of speaking one or the other of these primary words. But the two I's are not the same: 'The primary word *I–Thou* can only be spoken with the whole being. The primary word *I–It* can never be spoken with the whole being.' The real determinant of the primary word in which a man takes his stand is not the object over against him, but the way in which he relates himself to that object. I–Thou is the primary word of relationship. It is characterized by mutuality, directness, presentness, intensity, and ineffability. Although it is only within this relation that personality and the personal really exist, the Thou of I–Thou is not limited to men, but may include animals, trees, objects of nature, and God. I–It is the primary word of experiencing and using. It takes place within a man and not between him and the world. Hence it is entirely subjective and lacking in mutuality. Whether in knowing, feeling, or acting, it is the typical subject–object relationship. It is always mediate and indirect, dealing with objects in terms of the categories and connections, and hence is comprehensible and orderable. It is significant only in connection and not in itself. The It of I–It may equally well be a he, a she, an animal, a thing, a spirit, or even a god, without a change in the primary word. Thus I–Thou and I–It cut across the lines of our ordinary distinctions to focus our attention not upon individual objects and their causal connections, but upon the relations between things, the *dazwischen* ('there in-between'). Experiencing is I–It whether it is the experiencing of an object or of a man, whether it is 'inner' or 'outer', 'open' or 'secret'.

'The *It* is the eternal chrysalis, the *Thou* the eternal butter-fly.' What at one moment was the Thou of an I–Thou relation-ship can become the next moment an It and indeed must continually do so. The It may again become a Thou but it will not be able to remain one, and it need not become a Thou at all. Man can live continuously and securely in the world of It, but if he lives only in this world he is not a man.[1]

3

The starting-point of *I and Thou* is neither metaphysics nor theology but philosophical anthropology, the problem of man. Conversely, Buber's explicit philosophical anthropology, as it is developed in *Between Man and Man*, 'What Is Man?' (1938), and in the essays in this volume, is an extension and development of his philosophy of dialogue.

In 'What Is Man?' Buber defines 'philosophical anthropology' as the study of 'the *wholeness* of man', and he lists the following as among the problems 'which are implicitly set up at the same time by this question':

... man's special place in the cosmos, his connexion with destiny, his relation to the world of things, his understanding of his fellow men, his existence as a being that knows it must die, his attitude in the ordinary and extraordinary encounters with the mystery with which his life is shot through ...

The essence of man is determined by the fact that 'he shares in finitude and he shares in infinity':

Indissolubly connected with the finitude which is given by the ability to know *only* this, there is a participation in infinity, which is given by the ability to know at all. The meaning is therefore that when we recognize man's finitude we must *at the same time* recognize his participation in infinity, not as two juxtaposed qualities but as the twofold nature of the processes in which alone man's existence becomes recognizable.

The concern with the wholeness of man rules out the attempt

[1] Martin Buber, *I and Thou*, with a Postscript by the author, trans. by Ronald Gregor Smith (2nd ed.; New York: Charles Scribner's Sons, 1958), pp. 3, 5, 17 f., 34. (Edinburgh: T. & T. Clark, 1958).

to answer the question of what man is in terms of particular philosophical disciplines:

> Philosophy succeeds in rendering me . . . help in its individual disciplines precisely through each of these disciplines *not* reflecting, and not being able to reflect, on the wholeness of man. . . . in every one of these disciplines the possibility of its achieving anything in thought rests precisely on its objectification, on what may be termed its 'de-humanization'.

At the same time Buber disagrees with Martin Heidegger in his belief that philosophical anthropology can provide a foundation for metaphysics or for the individual philosophical sciences. If it tried to do this it would become so general that it would reach a false unity instead of the genuine wholeness of the subject based on 'the contemplation of all its manifold nature'.

> A legitimate philosophical anthropology must know that there is not merely a human species but also peoples, not merely a human soul but also types and characters, not merely a human life but also stages in life; only from the . . . recognition of the dynamic that exerts power within every particular reality and between them, and from the constantly new proof of the one in the many, can it come to see the wholeness of man.

Buber proceeds to set up philosophical anthropology as a systematic method which deals with the concrete, existential characteristics of man's life in order to arrive at the wholeness and uniqueness of man:

> Even as it must again and again distinguish within the human race in order to arrive at a solid comprehension, so it must put man in all seriousness into nature, it must compare him with other things, other living creatures, other bearers of consciousness, in order to define his special place reliably for him. Only by this double way of distinction and comparison does it reach the whole, real man, who, whatever his people or type or age, knows, what no being on earth but he can know, that he goes the narrow way from birth towards death, tests out what none

4

but he can, a wrestling with destiny, rebellion and reconciliation, and at times, even experiences in his own blood, when he is joined by choice to another human being, what goes on secretly in others.[1]

In defining philosophical anthropology as the problem of finding the human in the constant flux of individuals and cultures, Buber makes clear the one approach through which we can avoid the abyss of abstract unity, on the one hand, and that of meaningless relativity, on the other. In his definition of the problem, he has already given a twofold answer to the question of what man is: Man's existence is constituted by his participation, at the same time and in the same actions, in finitude and infinity; man's uniqueness is determined by the particular existential characteristics of his relation to 'mystery', cosmos, destiny, death, things, and man. Related to the definition of man as the creature who participates in both finitude and infinity is Buber's definition of man in *Between Man and Man* 'The Question to the Single One' as the only creature who has potentiality. 'Man', he writes, 'is the crystallized potentiality of existence.' Even though this wealth of possibility is confined within narrow limits, these limits are only factual and not essential. Man's action is unforeseeable in its nature and extent.[2] It is because of this potentiality that Buber is able to speak in terms of the freedom of man and the reality of evil. This potentiality also underlies his distinction between 'cosmological time', in which the future is determined as far as we are concerned, and 'anthropological time', in which the future is undetermined because it depends in part upon our decisions.[3]

A corollary of Buber's emphasis on the wholeness of man is his rejection of the traditional idea that reason is the distinctive human characteristic.

The depth of the anthropological question is first touched when we also recognize as specifically human that which is not reason. Man is not a centaur, he is man through and through.

[1] Martin Buber, *Between Man and Man*, trans. by Ronald Gregor Smith (Boston: Beacon Press, 1955), pp. 121–124; (London: Kegan Paul, 1947)

[2] *Ibid.*, pp. 77 f.   [3] *Ibid.*, 'What Is Man?', pp. 140 ff.

He can be understood only when one knows, on the one hand, that there is something in all that is human, including thought, which belongs to the general nature of living creatures, and is to be grasped from this nature, while knowing, on the other hand, that there is no human quality which belongs fully to the general nature of living creatures and is to be grasped exclusively from it. Even man's hunger is not an animal's hunger. Human reason is to be understood only in connexion with human non-reason. The problem of philosophical anthropology is the problem of a specific totality and of its specific structure.[1]

In 'What Is Man?' Buber defines man as the creature capable of entering into living relation with the world and things, with men both as individuals and as the many, and with 'the mystery of being—which is dimly apparent through all this but infinitely transcends it'. In a living relation with things, man not only regards them technically and purposively, but turns to them in their essential life. In an essential relation with men, similarly, one life opens to another 'so that one experiences the mystery of the other being in the mystery of one's own. The two participate in one another's lives in very fact, not psychically, but ontically'. This essential relation is not to be confused with Heidegger's category of solicitude for other men. Solicitude 'does not set a man's life in direct relation with the life of another', for in it one offers one's assistance but not oneself to the other person. An essential relation to God, finally, cannot be reached, as Kierkegaard thinks, 'by renunciation of the relation to the whole being', but must include all of one's encounters with the world and men.[2]

Buber concludes 'What Is Man?' with the statement that the uniqueness of man is to be found not in the individual, nor in the collective, but in the meeting of 'I' and 'Thou'.

The fundamental fact of human existence is neither the individual as such nor the aggregate as such. Each, considered by itself, is a mighty abstraction. The individual is a fact of existence in so far as he steps into a living relation with other

---

[1] Buber, *Between Man and Man*, 'What Is Man?', p. 160.
[2] *Ibid.*, pp. 161–181.

individuals. The aggregate is a fact of existence in so far as it is built up of living units of relation. . . . That essence of man which is special to him can be directly known only in a living relation. The gorilla, too, is an individual, a termitary, too, is a collective, but *I* and *Thou* exist only in our world because man exists, and the I, moreover, exists only through the relation to the *Thou*.

The sphere in which man meets man has been ignored because it possesses no smooth continuity. Its experience has been annexed to the soul and to the world, so that what happens to an individual can be distributed between outer and inner impressions. But when two individuals 'happen' to each other, then there is an essential remainder which is common to them, but which reaches out beyond the special sphere of each. That remainder is the basic reality, the 'sphere of the between' (*das Zwischenmenschliche*). 'The philosophical science of man, which includes anthropology and sociology, must take as its starting-point the consideration of this subject, "man with man".'[1]

4

Walter Blumenfeld, in a book based on Buber's 'What Is Man?', has criticized Buber's philosophical anthropology on the basis that one cannot 'objectively' determine the meaning of authentic existence in it, nor tell which of the possibilities of human existence is to be preferred. He suggests that in order to be accepted as valid Buber's anthropology would have to be grounded on empirical psychology and an objective and scientific hierarchy of values,[2] in other words on pure subject–object epistemology. In so doing he fails to see the integral relation between Buber's anthropology and his dialogical theory of knowledge. Although philosophical anthropology cannot replace the specific disciplines dealing with the study of man, neither can those disciplines be entirely separated from it. If

[1] Buber, *Between Man and Man*, 'What Is Man?', pp. 202–205.

[2] Walter Blumenfeld, *La Antropologia Filosofica de Martin Buber y la Filosofia Antropologica, Un Ensayo*, Vol. VI of Coleccion *Plena Luz, Pleno Ser* (Lima: Universidad Nacional, 1951), pp. 18–25, 97–102, 108–113, 120–126, 138, 141–150.

the basic purpose of the study of man is defined by the image of man as the creature who becomes what only he can become through confronting reality with his whole being, then the specific branches of that study must also include an understanding of man in this way, and this means not only as an object, but also, to begin with, as a Thou.

Blumenfeld also overlooks the distinction which Buber makes in 'What Is Man?' between the method of the psychologist and that of the anthropologist. Both face the difficulty, for example, that self-observation weakens the spontaneity of anger. The psychologist tries to meet this difficulty by remaining outside with the observing part of his being and yet letting his passion run its course. This makes his passion similar to that of the actor: the elemental outbreak is replaced by a release which is willed and as such is more emphasized, deliberate, and dramatic in its vehemence. The anthropologist, in contrast, 'can have nothing to do with a division of consciousness, since he has to do with the unbroken wholeness of events, and especially with the unbroken natural connection between feelings and actions'. The anthropologist, therefore, must let his anger rage to its conclusion without trying to gain a perspective; he allows the recollection of what he felt and did to take the place of psychological self-experience. His memory, like that of the great artists, has the concentrating power which preserves what is essential.

In the moment of life he has nothing else in his mind but just to live what is to be lived, he is there with his whole being, undivided, and for that very reason there grows in his thought and recollection the knowledge of human wholeness.[1]

When the Washington (D.C.) School of Psychiatry brought Martin Buber from Jerusalem in the spring of 1957 to give the William Alanson White Memorial Lectures, Fourth Series (all three of which are included in this volume), the title of these lectures was 'What Can Philosophical Anthropology Contribute to Psychiatry?' In his Introduction to these lectures, Dr Leslie H. Farber, Chairman of the Faculty of the Washington

[1] Buber, *Between Man and Man*, pp. 125 f.

School of Psychiatry, underscored Buber's contention that none of the sciences has asked the question about man in his *wholeness* that is the central concern of philosophical anthropology.

The medical and biological sciences were asking, What is man in his relation to nature—to natural history, the evolution of organisms, and the physical forces regulating his body? They were asking, What is man as a natural object, a physical or biological organism? And it was upon this natural basis that all the other sciences of man—anthropology, sociology, political science, and finally the new Freudian science of psychoanalysis —asked their question, What is man? What is the natural man, what is the primitive man, as opposed to the man created by socio-political, cultural, and economic forces? What is man in his natural inheritance, in his prehistory as the human animal or primate or primitive, as opposed to his more recent history as a civilized or social being? Thus none of the sciences were asking the *whole* question, What is man? Nor were they asking the unique question, Who am I, in my uniquely human essence? . . . These are not smaller or more personal questions; they are larger and more comprehensive than the ones which science has been asking. They include a larger view of man, as well as a larger view of history. They include man's personal being—*my* personal experience and knowledge of myself—as well as my philosophical and scientific knowledge of what '*man* is'. . . . Psychiatry must not close itself off from other disciplines—whether in philosophy or religion or moral science— which are equally absorbed with man and with the relations between men.[1]

Science investigates man not as a whole, but in selective aspects and as part of the natural world. Scientific method, in fact, is man's most highly perfected development of the I-It, or subject-object, way of knowing. Its methods of abstracting from the concrete actuality and of largely negating the inevitable difference between observers reduce the I in so far as possible to

[1] Leslie H. Farber, 'Introduction' to Martin Buber, 'The William Alanson White Memorial Lectures, Fourth Series', *Psychiatry*, XX, No. 2 (May 1957), 95 f.

the abstract knowing subject and the It in so far as possible to the passive and abstract object of thought. Just for these reasons scientific method is not qualified to discover the wholeness of man. It can compare men with each other and man with the animals, but from such comparison and contrast there can emerge only an expanding and contracting scale of similarities and differences. This scale, consequently, can be of aid in categorizing men and animals as differing objects in a world of objects, but not in discovering the uniqueness of man as man.

It may be objected by some that Buber's concern for man's wholeness prejudges the conclusions to be reached or that it is not a 'value-free' method. These objections are likely to be reinforced in the minds of those who make them by the qualifications which Buber sets for the philosophical anthropologist: that he must be an individual to whom man's existence as man has become questionable, that he must have experienced the tension of solitude, and that he must discover the wholeness of man not as a scientific observer, removed in so far as possible from the object that he observes, but as a participant who only afterward gains the distance from his subject matter which will enable him to formulate the insights he has attained.[1] Nonetheless, it is only the knowing of the I–Thou relation that makes possible the conception of the wholeness of man. Only I–Thou sees this wholeness as the whole person in unreserved relation with what is over against him rather than as a sum of parts, some of which are labelled objective and hence oriented around the thing known, and some subjective and hence oriented around the knower.

5

Martin Buber's philosophy of dialogue is not merely a phenomenological description of man's twofold attitude, but also an 'ontology' which points to 'the between' as the really real ('All real living is meeting'). In the last and decisive stage of his anthropology, however, Buber has found it necessary to deepen this ontological base by discovering the two basic movements of man from which the twofold principle of human

[1] Buber, *Between Man and Man*, pp. 124 f., 132 f., 180 f., 199 f.

life is derived. The clearest and most systematic treatment of this new stage is 'Distance and Relation', the essay that stands at the beginning of this volume and is the direct fountainhead of all the essays that follow. The first of these two movements Buber calls 'the primal setting at a distance', the second 'entering into relation'. The first movement is the presupposition for the second, for we can enter into relation only with being that has been set at a distance from us and thereby has become an independent opposite. Only through this act of setting at a distance does man have a 'world'—an unbroken continuum which includes not merely all that he and other men know and experience, but all that is knowable now or in the future. Buber characterizes the act of entering into relation with the world as 'synthesizing apperception', the apperception of a being as a whole and as a unity. This is done not simply through setting at a distance, but also through entering into relation. In human life together, it is the fact that man sets man at a distance and makes him independent that enables him to enter into relation, as an individual self, with those like himself. Through this 'interhuman' relation men confirm each other, becoming a self with the other. The inmost growth of the self is not induced by man's relation to himself, 'as people like to suppose today', but by the confirmation in which one man knows himself to be 'made present' in his uniqueness by the other. 'Self-realization', that vague shibboleth which occupies so large a place in our popular culture, is not the *goal* but the *by-product*. The goal is completing distance by relation, and relation here means mutual confirmation, co-operation, and genuine dialogue.

6

What is the connection between 'Distance and Relation' and Buber's philosophy of dialogue? In the Foreword to the German edition Buber writes, 'The connection . . . with my writings on dialogical existence is probably clear to the reader'. This is true in general but not as regards the particular links between 'distance' and 'relation', on the one hand, and 'I–Thou' and 'I–It', on the other. It is clear that 'entering into relation' means

11

entering into an I–Thou relationship, yet it is equally clear that one cannot identify distance with I–It. When man fails to enter into relation, however, the distance thickens and solidifies; instead of making room for relation it obstructs it. This failure to enter into relation corresponds to I–It, and distance thus becomes the presupposition for both I–Thou and I–It. Entering into relation is an act of the whole being: it is *the* act by which we constitute ourselves as human, and it is an act which must be repeated ever again in ever new situations. Distance, in contrast, is not an act, and neither is failure to enter into relation: both are states of being.

When Buber speaks in *I and Thou* of the I–Thou relationship as preceding the I–It in the primitive man and the child, he is speaking of the genesis of these relations. In 'Distance and Relation', on the other hand, he is speaking ontologically of what constitutes the human being as a human being. In this latter context there is no longer a distinction between 'primitive man' and 'civilized man' or between child and adult: Buber is not here interested in discovering just when, in the life of the race and the individual, man really becomes man, but only in discovering what makes up the uniqueness of man once he is man.

Even ontologically speaking, however, it might appear that if distance is the presupposition for relationship and I–It is the thickening of distance, then the I–It relation precedes rather than follows the I–Thou. This apparent contradiction rests on a misconception, namely, that the thickening of the distance is closer to the original situation than the entrance into relation. Distance is given to man as man, yet it is ontologically speaking pre-personal, that is, it precedes the I–Thou and I–It relations which make up personal existence. This distance given, man is able to enter into relation with other beings distant from, and opposed to, him, for the 'overcoming' of distance does not mean simple unity, but the polar tension of distance and relation together. Or, as we have seen, he is able to enlarge, develop, accentuate, and shape the distance itself. In this shaping of the distance the primary state of things is elaborated as it is not in I–Thou. The I–Thou relationship changes nothing in the primary state of things, but the thickening of distance into

I–It changes the whole situation of the other being, making it
into one's object. This applies to nonhuman as well as human,
inanimate as well as animate beings. Looking at and observing
the object, we make it part of an objective world with which
we do not enter into relationship. Hence the I–It, or subject–
object, relation is not the primary one, but is an elaboration
of the given as the I–Thou relationship is not.

In the actual development of the human person the I–Thou
relation does in fact precede the I–It, and entering into relation
precedes the thickening of distance that obstructs relationship.
The baby does not proceed directly from complete unity with
its mother to that primary I–Thou relation which Buber has
described in the child in the first part of *I and Thou*. Already
in its first days, according to Buber, a child has the fact of
distance, that is, the sense of beings as different from and over
against him. In entering into relationship with its mother the
child completes this distance, and it is only later when he ceases
to enter into relationship that he sees her as an object and falls
into I–It's shaping and elaboration of the distance.[1] This same
thing happens later when the child goes through the process of
emergence of the self. As consciousness of one's separateness
grows, it becomes more and more difficult to overcome the
distance through relation; heightened insecurity and need for
decision produce an ever greater temptation to accentuate the
distance and take refuge in the pseudo security of the world of
It, the world of ordered objectivity and private subjectivity.
Thus while I–It can be defined as the enlarging and thickening
of the distance, it can also be defined as the objectification of
the I–Thou relationship which sometimes serves as the way
back to it and sometimes obstructs the return.

Philosophizing and philosophy begin with a 'primary act of
abstraction', writes Buber, quoting Hegel—a definite looking
away from the concrete situation to the sphere of precise conceptualization. It is through this primary abstraction developed
in philosophizing that we possess an 'objective and self-
contained connection of all being, natural and spiritual'.

---

[1] I am indebted to Professor Buber for oral elucidation of these problems
during his first visit to America, 1951–1952.

Only through the fact that philosophy radically abandoned the relation with the concrete did that amazing establishment of an objective thought-continuum become possible with a static system of concepts and a dynamic one of problems.[1]

Here Buber is talking about the becoming of the developed world and not about its primary cause, which is, as we have seen, both man's setting at a distance and his entering into relationship. It might seem from this account, however, that Buber feels that the existence of a 'world' for man is directly dependent upon the philosophical extension of the I–It, or subject–object, relationship. This is not the case, however, as Buber makes clear when he criticizes Jean-Paul Sartre's statement that man 'should affirm himself as the being through whom a world exists'. 'That ordering of known phenomena which we call the world', writes Buber, 'is, indeed, the composite work of a thousand human generations.' But this world has come into existence through our meeting with existing being unknowable to us in its own nature. Though the becoming of a world takes place through us, our social ordering of the world rests, in its turn, on the priority of the meeting with existing being, and this meeting is not our work. 'What we call cosmos has its origin in the dialogue of the generations and not in philosophy.'[2] Hence here too entering into relation precedes the elaboration of distance—I–Thou precedes I–It.

The terminology of 'Distance and Relation' also clarifies the link between Buber's theory of knowledge and his ethics. The thickening of distance into I–It, which leads us to regard other existing beings as objects which we observe, also leads us to regard them as objects which are there for our use and exploitation. Observation and exploitation are two different stages of the same thing—the elaboration of the original situation into

---

[1] Martin Buber, *Eclipse of God. Studies in the Relation between Religion and Philosophy*, trans. by Maurice Friedman, *et al.* (New York: Harper & Row, 1957), 'Religion and Philosophy', pp. 38 f., 42 f; (London: Gollancz, 1953).

[2] *Ibid.*, 'Religion and Modern Thinking', pp. 68 f. The last sentence, in quotation marks, is from a letter by Martin Buber to me of Feb. 19, 1963, in which Buber stresses that one does not really possess a 'world' through abstraction but through the Heracleitian logos, or speech-with-meaning. (See my discussion of Buber's interpretation of Heracleitus in Section 9 of this essay.)

I–It. The *objective* observation which tries to see all things abstracted from the differences between subjective observers is only the prelude to the second stage of subjective use and exploitation.

7

'Distance and Relation' is the most important theoretical statement of the new stage that Buber's philosophy has reached in the essays in this book. 'Elements of the Interhuman', the essay that follows it, is the most important practical application of this stage to Buber's philosophy of dialogue and as such should be read not only in the sequence of these essays but as a complement to 'Dialogue' and the other essays on the life of dialogue in *Between Man and Man*. 'Elements of the Inter-human' carries forward in particular Buber's delineation of the 'sphere of the between' begun in 'What Is Man?' In 1905 Buber used the term *das Zwischenmenschliche* (a now familiar expression which he was the first to employ) as the social-psychological in general, 'the life of men together in all its forms and actions', 'the social seen as a psychological process'. A half-century later, in 'Elements of the Interhuman', he restricted the use of the term to that in human life which provides the basis for direct dialogical relations. In distinction to the 'interhuman' Buber now sets the sphere of the 'social' in which many individual existences are bound into a group with common experiences and reactions, but without any personal relation necessarily existing between one person and another within the group. In an era in which the direction of groups in general has been toward the suppression of the elements of personal relation in favour of the elements of pure collectivity, this distinction is of the greatest importance. Even Carl Jung, a psychologist who was concerned for most of his life with the inner life of man, recognized in one of his latest writings the threat of collectivization to the interhuman:

The mass State has no intention of promoting mutual under-standing and the relationship of man to man; it strives, rather, for atomization, for the psychic isolation of the individual. The

15

more unrelated individuals are, the more consolidated the State becomes, and vice versa. . . . The question of human relationship and of the inner cohesion of our society is an urgent one in view of the atomization of the pent-up mass man, whose personal relationships are undermined by general mistrust.[1]

The distinction between the 'social' and the 'interhuman' is also of great significance in an intellectual climate in which the importance of 'interpersonal relations' and the 'social self' are increasingly recognized and at the same time are indiscriminately confused with 'dialogue' and the 'I–Thou' relationship. The 'social' includes the I–It relation as well as the I–Thou: Many interpersonal relations are really characterized by one person's treating the other as an object to be known and used. Most interpersonal relations are, in fact, a mixture of I–Thou and I–It and some almost purely I–It. Both George Herbert Mead and Harry Stack Sullivan include something of what Buber calls the 'interhuman' in their treatment of the social self and the interpersonal, but, unlike Buber, neither man singles out the interhuman as a separate dimension, qualitatively different and essentially significant.

The unfolding of the sphere of 'the between' Buber calls the 'dialogical'. The psychological, that which happens within the souls of each, is only the secret accompaniment to the dialogue. The meaning of this dialogue is found in neither one nor the other of the partners, nor in both added together, but in their interchange. This distinction between the 'dialogical' and the 'psychological' constitutes a radical attack on the psychologism of our age. It makes manifest the fundamental ambiguity of those modern psychologists who affirm the dialogue between man and man, but who are unclear as to whether this dialogue is of value in itself or is merely a function of the individual's self-acceptance and self-realization. 'Individuation is only the indispensable personal stamp of all realization of human existence', writes Buber in 'Elements of the Interhuman'. 'The self as such is not ultimately the essential, but the meaning of human existence given in creation again and again fulfils itself

---

[1] *The Undiscovered Self*, trans. by R. F. C. Hull (Boston: Little, Brown & Co., 1957), pp. 103–106; (London: Routledge, 1958)

as self.' By pointing to dialogue as the intrinsic value and self-realization as only the corollary and by-product rather than the goal, Buber also separates himself from those theologians and existential psychotherapists who tend to make the I–Thou relationship just another dimension of the self, along with one's relation to oneself and to one's environment.

The interhuman is the I–Thou relationship in so far as the latter refers to the dialogue between man and man. It is not synonymous with that relationship, however, since according to *I and Thou* man can also have an I–Thou relationship with nature and with art. In 'Elements of the Interhuman', however, Buber has emphasized the difference between our knowledge of other persons and our knowledge of things as he has not in *I and Thou*. This does not mean that he rejects the I–Thou relation with nature and art, but as he once told me, if he were to write *I and Thou* again, he would seek different categories to make clearer the distinction between these latter types of I–Thou relationships and the dialogue between man and man. We have in common with every thing the ability to become an object of observation, writes Buber in 'Elements', but it is the privilege of man, through the hidden action of his being, to be able to impose an insurmountable limit to his objectification. Only as a partner can man be perceived as an existing wholeness. To become aware of a man means to perceive his wholeness as person defined by spirit: to perceive the dynamic centre which stamps on all his utterances, actions, and attitudes the tangible sign of oneness. Such an awareness is impossible if, and so long as, the other is for me, for example, the detached object of my observation, for he will not thus yield his wholeness and its centre. It is possible only when he becomes present for me.

The essential problematic of the sphere of the between, writes Buber, is the duality of being and seeming. The man dominated by being gives himself to the other spontaneously without thinking about the image of himself awakened in the beholder. The 'seeming man', in contrast, is primarily concerned with what the other thinks of him, and produces a look calculated to make himself appear 'spontaneous', 'sincere', or whatever he thinks will win the other's approval. This 'seeming' destroys the authenticity of the life between man and man and thus the authenticity of human existence in general. The tendency toward seeming originates in man's need for confirmation and in his desire to be confirmed falsely rather than not to be confirmed at all. To give in to this tendency is the real cowardice of man, writes Buber; to withstand it his real courage.

This distinction between 'being man' and 'seeming man' is central to Buber's anthropology, for it enables him to substitute for the older notions of man's being good or bad by nature the more modern realization that even though some men appear to be entirely determined by seeming, it is only the successive layers of deception that give the illusion of individuals who are seeming men by their very nature. 'I have never known a young person who seemed to me irretrievably bad', writes Buber. 'Man is, as man, redeemable.' This distinction is important further because it links 'Elements of the Inter-human' with one of the most significant developments in Buber's thought, namely, the gradually growing stress on the importance of a 'personal making present' of the other as the basis of that 'confirmation' through which we are enabled to become what we are called to become. In 'Education' (1926)[1] Buber has already dealt with this subject in the form of the trust of the child in the adult who remains truly present to the child through gathering 'the child's presence into his own store as one of the bearers of his communion with the world, one of the focuses of his responsibilities for the world'. He also discusses it as 'inclusion', that 'experiencing the other side' of the relationship that enables one, without losing anything of his own reality, to live through the common event from the standpoint of the other'. 'Experiencing the other side' is only one kind, the most significant indeed, of what Buber calls 'making present'. In 'Distance and Relation', as we have seen, Buber sees this mutual confirmation as essential to becoming a self—a person who realizes his uniqueness precisely through his relation to other selves whose distance from him is completed by his distance from them.

True confirmation means that I confirm my partner as this existing being even while I oppose him. I legitimize him over

[1] Later published in *Between Man and Man*.

against me as the one with whom I have to do in real dialogue. This mutual confirmation of men is most fully realized in what Buber calls 'making present', an event which happens partially wherever men come together, but in its essential structure only rarely. Making the other present means 'to imagine the real', to imagine quite concretely what another man is wishing, feeling, perceiving, and thinking. This is no empathy or intuitive perception, but a bold swinging into the other which demands the intensest action of one's being, even as does all genuine fantasy; only here the realm of one's act 'is not the all-possible' but the particular, real person who steps up to meet one, the person whom one seeks to make present as just so and not otherwise in all his wholeness, unity, and uniqueness. One can only do this as a partner, standing in a common situation with the other, and even then one's address to the other may remain unanswered and the dialogue may die in seed.

Buber's teaching of confirmation is of the greatest importance for his philosophy of dialogue in general and for its application to family life, education, and psychotherapy in particular. To appreciate its importance we must make a distinction that many have failed to make and that Buber himself only makes explicit in the dialogue with the psychologist Carl R. Rogers that is printed as the Appendix to this volume. This is the distinction between acceptance, or affirmation, of the other and 'confirmation'. In this dialogue (which I had the privilege of moderating at the University of Michigan in the spring of 1957) Rogers emphasizes an unqualified acceptance of the person being helped, whereas Buber emphasizes a confirmation which, while it accepts the other as a person, may also wrestle *with* him against himself. In his stress on acceptance, Rogers says that if the therapist is willing for the other person to *be what he is*—'to possess the feelings he possesses, the hold the attitudes he holds'—it will help him to realize what is 'deepest in the individual, that is the very aspect that can most be trusted to be constructive or to tend toward socialization or toward the development of better inter-personal relationships'. In his reply Buber sees man, in contrast, as neither good nor evil by nature, but as polar:

What you say may be trusted, I would say this stands in polar relation to what can be least trusted in this man. . . . When I grasp him more broadly and more deeply than before, I see his whole polarity and then I see how the worst in him and the best in him are dependent on one another, attached to one another.

This doctrine of polarity leads inevitably to Buber's distinction between acceptance and confirmation. Rogers speaks of acceptance as a warm regard for the other and a respect for him as a person of unconditional worth, and that means 'an acceptance of and regard for his attitudes of the moment, no matter how much they may contradict other attitudes he has held in the past'. In response to my question as to whether he would not distinguish confirmation from acceptance of this sort, Buber says:

I not only accept the other as he is, but I confirm him, in myself, and then in him, in relation to this potentiality that is meant by him and it can now be developed, it can evolve, it can answer the reality of life. . . . Let's take, for example, man and wife. He says, not expressly, but just by his whole relation to her, 'I accept you as you are'. But thus does *not* mean 'I don't want you to change'. But it says, 'I discover in you just by my accepting love, I discover in you what you are meant to become'.

Rogers, in turn, recognizes that we could not accept the individual as he is 'because often he is in pretty sad shape, if it were not for the fact that we also in some sense realize and recognize his potentiality'. But he goes on to stress the acceptance as that which makes for the realization of potentiality: 'Acceptance of the most complete sort, acceptance of this person as he is, is the strongest factor making for change that I know.' To this Buber replies, speaking of the problematic type with which 'I have necessarily to do':

There are cases when I must help him against himself. He wants my help against himself. . . . The first thing of all is that he trusts me. . . . What he wants is a being not only whom he can trust as a man trusts another, but a being that gives him now the certitude that 'there *is* a soil, there *is* an existence'. And if this is reached, now I can help this man even in his struggle against himself. And this I can only do if I distinguish between accepting and confirming.

The issue between Martin Buber and Carl R. Rogers also concerns the therapist–patient relationship: Must it be based on a one-sided inclusion, as Buber holds, or on full mutuality at every level, as Rogers claims? In friendship and love, 'inclusion', or experiencing the other side, is mutual. In the helping relationships, however, it is, says Buber, necessarily one-sided. The patient cannot equally well experience the relationship from the side of the therapist or the pupil from the side of the teacher without destroying or fundamentally altering the relationship. This does not mean that the therapist, for example, is reduced to treating his patient as an object, an It. The one-sided inclusion of therapy is still an I–Thou relationship founded on mutuality, trust, and partnership in a common situation, and it is only in this relation that real therapy can take place. If 'all real living is meeting', as Buber says in *I and Thou*, all true healing also takes place through meeting.

If the psychotherapist is satisfied to 'analyse' the patient, 'i.e. to bring to light unknown factors from his microcosm, and to set to some conscious work in life the energies which have been transformed by such an emergence', then, says Buber in his 1958 Postscript to *I and Thou*, he may be successful in some repair work. At best he may help a soul which is diffused and poor in structure to collect and order itself to some extent. But the real matter, the regeneration of an atrophied personal centre, will not be achieved. This can be done only by one who grasps the buried latent unity of the suffering soul with the great glance of the doctor: and this can only be attained in the person-to-person attitude of a partner, not by the consideration and examination of an object.

A common situation, however, does not mean one which each enters from the same or even a similar position. In psychotherapy the difference in position is not only that of personal stance, but of role and function, a difference determined by the very difference of purpose which led each to enter the relationship. If the goal is a common one—the healing of the patient—the relationship to that goal differs radically as between therapist and patient, and the healing that takes place depends as much upon the recognition of that difference as upon the mutuality of meeting and trust.

In order that he may coherently further the liberation and actualisation of that unity in a new accord of the person with the world, the psychotherapist, like the educator, must stand again and again not merely at his own pole in the bipolar relation, but also with the strength of present realisation at the other pole, and experience the effect of his own action. . . . the specific 'healing' relation would come to an end the moment the patient thought of, and succeeded in, practising 'inclusion' and experiencing the event from the doctor's pole as well. Healing, like educating, is only possible to the one who lives over against the other, and yet is detached.[1]

The I–Thou relationship must always be understood in terms of the quite concrete situation and life-reality of those participating in it. Here the full reality of the concrete situation includes the fact that one is a sick man who has come to the therapist for help, the other a therapist who is ready to enter a relationship in order to help. This excludes neither Erich Fromm's conviction that the therapist at the same time heals himself in some measure through his own response to the patient, nor Carl R. Rogers' feeling of the equal worth and value of the client (which leads Rogers, mistakenly in my opinion, to stress the full mutuality of the client–therapist relationship). But it does preclude accepting the therapist's *feeling* of mutuality as equivalent to the actual existence of full mutuality in the situation *between* therapist and patient. The 'scientific' impersonalism that characterized the orthodox conception of the psychoanalyst is rightly rejected by many present-day therapists. But this should not lead us to a sentimental blurring of the essential distinction between therapy

[1] Buber, *I and Thou*, p. 133.

22

and other, less structured types of I–Thou relationships. In the latter, as Buber puts it, there are 'no normative limitations of mutuality', but in the former the very nature of the relationship makes full mutuality impossible.

8

In 'Healing through Meeting' (1952) Martin Buber throws out a hint concerning the nature of 'the unconscious' which is nowhere elaborated in his other writings:

The sphere in which this renowned concept possesses reality is located, according to my understanding, beneath the level where human existence is split into physical and psychical phenomena. But each of the contents of this sphere can in any moment enter into the dimension of the introspective, and thereby be explained and dealt with as belonging to the psychic province.[1]

In March and April of 1957 Buber conducted seven private seminars for the Washington School of Psychiatry, in addition to delivering the three public lectures which are included in this volume ('Distance and Relation', 'Elements of the Inter-human', and 'Guilt and Guilt Feelings'). Three of these seminars dealt with the unconscious, a subject on which Buber had devoted much study and thought and on which he later intended to write an essay for this volume. This topic is an essential part of Buber's anthropology and is one that has revolutionary implications for the understanding of 'what philosophical anthropology can contribute to psychiatry'—the over-all title of Buber's William Alanson White Memorial Lectures. It is doubly unfortunate, therefore, that Buber has been unable to write this essay. Agreeing to its importance, however, he has consented that I discuss his views of the unconscious on the basis of the notes which I and others took at these seminars.

Freud, said Buber, fell into the logical fallacy of declaring

[1] *Pointing the Way: Collected Essays*, ed. and trans. with Introductory Essay by Maurice Friedman (New York: Harper & Row (Torchbook), 1963), 'Healing through Meeting', p. 94; (London: Routledge, 1957).

the unconscious to be psychical as the alternative to the view of his opponents, who held that because the psyche is conscious the unconscious must be physiological. To recognize that the unconscious is *not* only physiological does not necessarily mean that it is *only* psychical, yet Freud and all those who have followed him in the various schools of psychiatry have held this to be the case. Revolutionary as are Jung's differences from Freud, he too puts the unconscious into the *psychical* category, and so does all modern psychology.

The *physical* and the *psychical* represent two radically different modes of knowing: that of the senses and that of the 'inner sense'. Pure psychic process is not to be found in the physical. Our memory retains the process, to be sure, but by a new process in time. Physiology deals with things that are to be found, psychology with things that are not to be found. The psychic is pure process in time. In order to grasp the physical as a whole, we need the category of space as well as time. But for the psychic we need time alone. There are meeting points between the physical and the psychical—conscious ones—but we must distinguish between these two articulations of the unconscious.

The assumption that the unconscious is either body or soul, physical or psychical, is unfounded. The unconscious is a state out of which these two phenomena have not yet evolved and in which the two cannot at all be distinguished from one another. The unconscious is our being itself in its wholeness. Out of it the physical and the psychical evolve again and again and at every moment. The unconscious is not a phenomenon. The unconscious is what modern psychology holds it to be—a dynamic fact which makes itself felt by its effects, effects which the psychologist can explore. But this exploration, as it takes place in psychiatry, is not of the unconscious itself but of the phenomena that have been dissociated from it. Modern psychology's claim that there are unconscious things which influence our life and come out in certain conscious states is one that Buber, in contrast to Sartre, Ludwig Binswanger, and other phenomenologists, does not contest. But we cannot, he reminds us, say anything about the unconscious in itself. It is never given to us. The radical mistake that Freud made was to think that he could posit a region of the mind as unconscious and at the same time deal with it as if its 'contents' were simply conscious material which was repressed and which could be brought back, without any essential change, into the conscious.

Dissociation is the process in which the unconscious 'lump' manifests itself in inner and outer perceptions. This dissociation, in fact, may be the origin of our whole sense of inner and outer. The conscious life of the patient is a dualistic life, as he knows it; his objective life is not dualistic, but he does not know this life. Man can have in a certain measure the consciousness, the coming together of his forces, his acting unity, but he cannot perceive his unity as an object.

If the unconscious is not of the nature of the psychic, then it follows that the basic distinction between the physical and the psychic as 'outer' and 'inner' does not apply to the unconscious. Yet Freud, holding that the unconscious must be simply psychical, places the unconscious *within* the person alone, and so do all the schools that have come after Freud. As a result, the basis of human reality itself comes to be seen as psychical rather than interhuman, and the relations between man and man are psychologized. The positing by most psychological schools of a nonphenomenological yet psychical reality means the assumption of a quasi-mystical basis of reality. Only from our continuous life-experience do we know about being— comprehending the two kinds of phenomena, the physical and the psychic. The assumption of an unconscious psyche that exists as something exists in space is either a metaphor or an entirely metaphysical thesis about the nature of being for which we have no basis at all in experience.

On this view of the unconscious, we must also say, in contrast to Freud, that we do not know dreams at all. We do not *have* a dream as we have some physical object. What we have, rather, is the work of 'shaping memory'. What this shaping memory gives us is not a reality that we dreamed, but rather a new reality produced by our attitude in relation to x—the 'dream' that we can never know in itself. We must question, therefore, the concept of the 'content' of dreams and with it Freud's whole theory of repression.

We are inclined to think that the rhythmical recurrence of

dreams is analogous to the conscious state of the soul. Yet in reality we cannot compare a dream to any other phenomenon. There is in conscious life an ordering force. Each morning anew when we awake a power begins to make us act and live in a common cosmos. Nothing of this kind happens in dreams. They have a certain continuity and connection of their own, but we cannot understand this connection or compare it to that of the waking world. The dream is not given us as an object of investigation. The dreamer, so long as he is dreaming, has no share in the common world and nothing, therefore, to which we can have access.

What is true of dreams is true of the unconscious in general. The unconscious is not something psychical that can be preserved in the underground, but just a piece of human body-and-soul existence: it cannot at all be raised again as it was. We do not have a deep freeze which retains psychical fragments that may be delivered up intact to the conscious. The unconscious has its own existence, which can again be dissociated into physical and psychic phenomena, but this dissociaton means a radical change of substance. This radical change can be brought about by the patient under the supervision, help, and even initiative of the therapist. This new dissociation can be accomplished in very different ways—recalling dreams, free association, memory of past events—but in each of these ways a radical change takes place.

Even the concept of 'transference' changes radically if we no longer mean by it making the unconscious conscious but rather the elaboration of elements that are dissociated from the unconscious. If the aim of therapy is to bring up something that is lying in the underground of the unconscious, then the therapist is only a kind of midwife. But if this work means the real and sometimes radical change of the substance, then transference eminently implies a certain influence of the therapist on the very act that is taking place. The patient feels as if he were discovering something that is going on which is essentially the same as what is contained in his soul in unconscious form. Actually this is not the case. He brings up what he senses is wanted of him, something which is the product of his relationship with the therapist.

Since the material that the patient brings forth in therapy is made and produced rather than simply brought up from the unconscious, the responsibility of the therapist is greater than has been supposed. 'In the last ten years or so', said Buber in the course of one of the 1957 seminars, 'I have the impression of a certain change in psychotherapeutic practice in which more and more therapists are not so confident that this or that theory is right and have a more "musical", floating relationship to their patients. The deciding reality is the therapist, not the methods.' Although no doctor can do without a typology, he knows that at a certain moment the unique person of the patient stands before the unique person of the doctor. He throws away as much of his typology as he can and accepts the unforeseeable happening that goes on between therapist and patient. Although one is not allowed to renounce either typology or method, one must know at what moments one should put them aside.

'There are two kinds of therapists', said Buber, 'one who knows more or less consciously the kind of interpretation of dreams he will get; and the other, the psychologist who does not know. I am entirely on the side of the latter, who does not want something precise. He is ready to receive what he will receive. He cannot know what method he will use beforehand. He is, so to speak, in the hands of his patient.' One cannot interpret poetry by the same methods as a novel, and still less can one interpret the dreams of one patient by the same methods as the dreams of another. A man is a better therapist if in the interpretation of dreams he is not a Freudian, Jungian, or Adlerian, but is guided by what the patient brings to him. The therapist must be ready to be surprised. From this type of 'obedient listening' a new type of therapist may evolve—a person of greater responsibility and even greater gifts, since it is not so easy to master new attitudes without ready-made categories.

The usual therapist imposes himself on his patient without being aware of it. What is necessary is the conscious liberation of the patient from this unconscious imposition of the therapist —leaving the patient really to himself and seeing what comes out of it. The therapist approaches the patient, but he must try

27

to influence him as little as possible, i.e., the patient must not be influenced by the general ideas of the school. 'It is much easier to impose oneself on the patient than it is to use the whole force of one's soul to leave the patient to himself and not to touch him. The real master responds to uniqueness.'

If the unconscious is that part of the existence of a person in which the realm of body and soul are not dissociated, then the relationship between two persons would mean the relationship between two nondivided existences. Thus the highest moment of relation would be what we call unconscious. The unconscious should have, may have, and indeed will have more influence in the interhuman than the conscious. In shaking hands, for example, if there is a real desire to be in touch, the contact is not bodily or psychical, but a unity of one and the other. There is a direct contact between persons in their wholeness, of which the unconscious is the guardian.

In the time of the strongest transference the patient needs in his unconscious to give himself up into the hands of the therapist so that contact may arise between them. The therapist's openness and willingness to receive whatever comes is necessary in order that the patient may trust existentially. A certain very important kind of healing—existential healing—takes place through meeting rather than through insight and analysis. This means healing not just of a certain part of the patient, but of the very roots of the patient's being. The existential trust of one whole person to another has a particular representation in the domain of healing. So long as it is not there, there will be no realization of this need to give up into the hands of the therapist what is repressed. Without such trust even masters of method cannot succeed in existential healing.

The existential trust between therapist and patient which makes the relationship a healing one in the fullest sense of that term implies confirmation, but of a very special sort. Such confirmation does not replace transference, but where meeting is the decisive factor, it changes its meaning and dynamic. Everything is changed in real meeting. Confirmation can be misunderstood as *static*. I meet another—I accept and confirm him as he now is. But confirming a person *as he is* is only the first step. Confirmation does not mean that I take his appearance at this moment as being the person I want to confirm. I must take the other person in his dynamic existence, in his specific potentiality. In the present lies hidden what *can become*. This potentiality, this sense of his unique direction as a person, can make itself felt to me within our relationship, and it is that which I most want to confirm. In therapy this personal direction becomes perceptible to the therapist in a very special way. In the strongest illness that appears in the life of a person, the highest potentiality of this person may be manifesting itself in negative form. The therapist can directly influence the development of those potentialities. Healing does not mean bringing up the old, but shaping the new: it is not confirming the negative, but counterbalancing with the positive.

9

'What Is Common to All' represents an important theoretical expansion of the concept of the 'essential We' that Buber set forth in 'What Is Man?' This concept is basic to Buber's anthropology and is an important corrective to that emphasis on the I–Thou relationship that has led many people, who are familiar with Buber's philosophy of dialogue but not his social philosophy, to the mistaken notion that Buber's thought is limited to the relation between one person and another and does not encompass the larger realities of community living. In 'What Is Man?' Buber designates a category of the 'essential We' to correspond on the level of the relation to a host of men to the 'essential *Thou* on the level of self-being'. He distinguishes this 'essential We' from the 'primitive We', 'to which the essential *We* is related in the same way as the essential *Thou* to the primitive *Thou*'. As the 'primitive Thou' precedes the consciousness of individual separateness, whereas the 'essential Thou' follows and grows out of this consciousness, so the 'primitive We' precedes true individuality and independence, whereas the 'essential We' only comes about when independent people have come together in essential relation and directness. The essential We includes the Thou potentially, for 'only men who are capable of truly saying *Thou* to one another can truly say *We* with one another'. Through this essential We and only through it can man escape from the impersonal 'one' (*das Man*) of the nameless, faceless crowd. 'A man is truly saved from the "one" not by separation but only by being bound up in genuine communion.'[1]

The essential We is not of secondary or merely instrumental importance; it is basic to existence, and as such it is itself a prime source of value. In contrast to Martin Heidegger, who interprets the logos of Heracleitus as the *individual* relationship to being which, prior to all speech, discloses being in existence,[2] Buber, in 'What Is Common to All', finds in his interpretation of Heracleitus the very base for his teaching of the essential We. Buber quotes Heracleitus, 'One should follow the common' —i.e., join with others in building a common world of speech and a common order of being. 'Man has always had his experiences as I, his experiences with others and with himself; but it is as We, ever again as We that he has constructed and developed a world out of his experiences.' Thus amid the changes of world images, 'the human cosmos is preserved, guarded by its moulder, the human speech-with-meaning, the common logos'.

The importance of Buber's concept of the common world as built by the common speech-with-meaning can hardly be over-estimated. Speech, from this point of view, is no mere function or tool. It is itself of the stuff of reality, able to create or destroy it. 'Man has always thought his thoughts as I, ... but as We he has ever raised them into being itself, in just that mode of existence that I call "the between".' Speech may be falsehood and conventionality, but it is also the great pledge of truth. Whether he takes refuge in individualism or collectivism, the man who flees answering for the genuineness of his existence is marked, writes Buber, by the fact that he can no longer really listen to the voice of another. The other is now only his object that he observes. But true dialogue, as Franz Rosenzweig pointed out, means that the other has not only ears but a mouth. He can say something that will surprise one, something new, unique, and unrepeatable for which the only adequate reply is

[1] Buber, *Between Man and Man*, pp. 175 ff.
[2] Martin Heidegger, *An Introduction to Metaphysics* (New York: Doubleday Anchor Books, 1961), pp. 106–115; (Oxford University Press, 1959).

the spontaneous response of the whole being and nothing that can be prepared beforehand. Only if real listening as well as real talking takes place will the full possibility of learning be present in class discussions, the full possibility of healing be present in group psychotherapy. Only through genuine listening, and not through any mere *feeling* of group unity, will the full potentiality of any group as a group be realized. 'He who existentially knows no Thou will never succeed in knowing a We.' One *should* follow the common, which means that lived speech, speech-with-meaning, is a value in itself. Values are not just the content, the building-blocks of speech. They exist, in the realest sense, in 'the between', in the dialogue between man and man. The value of speech depends upon genuine dialogue, but it does not depend upon agreement or simple understanding. On the contrary, as Buber points out in 'The Word That Is Spoken', misunderstanding is itself fruitful as the ground upon which ever new, genuinely two-sided understanding may take place.

It is not only the fate of groups and communities that depends upon the common speech-with-meaning. If man does not recover the genuineness of existence as We, writes Buber in 'What Is Common to All', he may cease to exist at all:

In our age, in which the true meaning of every word is encompassed by delusion and falsehood and the original intention of the human glance is stifled by tenacious mistrust, it is of decisive importance to find again the genuineness of speech and existence as We. . . . Man will not persist in existence if he does not learn anew to persist in it as a genuine We.

In Buber's critique of the mystical teaching of identity in 'What Is Common to All', we find an important clue to one of the most difficult and important questions in understanding Buber's ethics, namely, whether the base of his ethics is specifically religious, i.e., connected with historical revelation, or whether it is his philosophical anthropology, and as such religious only in the broader definition that Buber gives the term when he speaks of it as concerning the totality of man's existence rather than any special province of it. In 'What Is

Common to All' Buber sets Heracleitus' injunction, 'One should follow the common', in contrast to Taoist, Hindu, and modern mystical teachings, which he characterizes as a flight from 'the arch reality out of which all community stems—human meeting'. By denying the uniqueness of the human person these teachings annihilate it, one's own person as well as the other; for human existence and the intercourse of men that grows out of it is the chance for meeting in which each says to the other not 'I am you', but 'I accept you as you are'. 'Here first is uncurtailed existence.'

That Buber's basis for this distinction between Heracleitus and the Eastern teachings is his anthropology, with its conception of authentic existence, rather than his philosophy of religion as such, is made clear by his criticism of Aldous Huxley's counsel to the use of the mescalin drug:

Man may master as he will his situation, to which his surroundings also belong; he may withstand it, he may alter it, he may, when it is necessary, exchange it for another; but the fugitive flight out of the claim of the situation into situationlessness is no legitimate affair of man. And the true name of all paradises which man creates for himself by chemical or other means is situationless-ness.

Even the mystic who turns away from existence as We to a deepened contemplation of existing being is still fleeing from the 'leaping fire' with which, in his Seventh Epistle, according to Buber, Plato describes the dynamic between persons in We.

The flight from the common cosmos into a special sphere that is understood as the true being is, in all its stages, from the elemental sayings of the ancient Eastern teachings to the arbitrariness of the modern counsel to intoxication, a flight from the existential claim on the person who must authenticate himself in We. It is a flight from the authentic spokenness of speech in whose realm a response is demanded, and response is responsibility.

It is particularly remarkable that Buber does *not* rest his case against the Taoist, Vedantist, and modern mystic on any religious grounds, since we are confronted here with basic differences in the understanding of reality, meaning, and value that are, in the last instance, religious in nature: no nondualist Vedantist would be troubled by Buber's criticism because for him true 'personal' existence and the true We are found precisely on the road that Buber holds annihilates them. On the other hand, the common logos of speech and response is grounded much more securely in the biblical view of existence as the dialogue between man and God than in Heracleitus' concept of a reality that 'was and is and ever shall be everliving Fire'. Buber himself recognizes this limitation to the possibility of enregistering Heracleitus' teaching of the common in the 'life of dialogue':

> What he designates as the common has nothing that is over against it as such: logos and cosmos are, to him, self-contained; there is nothing that transcends them. . . . No salvation is in sight for us, however, if we are not able again 'to stand before the face of God' in all reality as a We.

Buber does not explain wherein the common logos and cosmos of Heracleitus is lacking—as dialogue, as authentic existence itself, in its historical dimension, or in the dimension of religious revelation. Nonetheless, we may conclude that Buber is here recognizing that the ultimate, even if not the immediate, base for his view of authentic existence and for the anthropology in which it is set is religious. Real existence as a We is not possible in a self-contained cosmos, but only in ever renewed dialogue with what is over against us. Although we exist as We through actual and potential relationships between person and person, the We too must sometimes be like an I: to find its own true existence, it too has to enter into relation with the Thou that confronts it—the Thou of other nations, of history, of God.[1]

Buber's critique of Huxley's counsel to the use of mescalin is of specifically modern importance, apart from its links with

[1] For a fullscale treatment of the relation of Buber's anthropology and his philosophy of religion as bases of his ethics see my essay, 'The Bases of Buber's Ethics' in Paul Arthur Schilpp and Maurice Friedman, eds., *The Philosophy of Martin Buber*, volume in 'The Library of Living Philosophers' (La Salle, Ill.: The Open Court Publishing Co., 1965).

the mystical doctrines of the past. Huxley recommends mescalin as a means to acquire insight into what the mystics of all the ages experienced. But the mystics of the ages, Buber points out, were men who were seized on their way by their mystical experiences, not men who arbitrarily set out to have such experiences. This critique applies not only to Huxley vis-à-vis the mystics, but to the whole modern cult of experience, especially as it applied to religion. When William James wrote *Varieties of Religious Experience*, he was, for an empirical scientist, phenomenally open to the whole range of phenomena of religious experience. Yet he set the fashion, at the same time, for extracting the mystical 'experience' from the whole religious reality and context of which it is an inseparable part. This extraction not only falsifies religious reality by turning it into a psychological content—an experience that a person *has*; it also leads to the pragmatic inversion that causes James and Huxley to encourage others to cultivate these experiences so that they too may know these 'real effects'. The great mystics did not *have* experiences, they *were had* by them. They were seized by them in their total being and just thereby knew themselves to be in contact with a larger reality than themselves. The modern cultivator of experience, in contrast, knows no truly independent reality since 'experience' has become for him something he possesses, an internal, essentially psychological reality whose effects on him are far more real than the source of these effects. It follows, by the same token, that he does not 'experience' with his whole being, but only with that part of him which registers the effects, while the other part of him, the one that seeks the experience, remains perforce the detached observer separated from his experience by his very knowledge that he is having it. As a result, the spontaneity of total religious reality is replaced by double-mindedness in the whole range of 'religious experience' from prayer and spiritual training to the use of mescalin and lycurgic acid: Modern man's overconsciousness that *he* is praying, his 'holding back of an I which does not enter into the action with the rest of the person', takes away the spontaneity which is the presupposition of genuine prayer.[1]

[1] Buber, *Eclipse of God*, 'God and the Spirit of Man', p. 126.

Huxley's reduction of both the human and the mystical to the visual leaves out that whole aspect of human existence and of religious reality that comes with hearing and answering the word. Huxley is not unaware of the sense of hearing, of course, but he reduces it to a secondary place, making reality ultimately visual in nature, and he does so by means of the fallacious notion that the visual is direct while the auditory, and in particular the word, is mediate and indirect. The dialectic between the mediate and the immediate which is the very heart of the word as it is taken up into lived speech is ignored by Huxley.

10

The central significance and meaning of lived speech for human existence is elaborated by Buber in 'The Word That Is Spoken'. The concern of the modern logical analyst for clarification of concepts is not new. In Western thought it goes back to Socrates and in Eastern to Confucius. There is a story in Confucius' *Analects*, remarked Buber at the opening of the seminars on the Unconscious, about a disciple who spent some time at the court of one of the kings 'clearing up designations'. As long as they are unclear, everything in the kingdom is doubtful. What makes designations problematic is not, as so many think, because there are no single, agreed-on definitions. 'They are problematic because they do not show a concrete context that can be controlled. Every abstraction must stand the test of being related to a concrete reality without which it has no meaning. This revision of designations entails a necessary destruction if the new generation is not to be the life-long slave of tradition.'

Our goal is not agreement or unanimity. We clarify designations only in order that we may discuss them, and relate to each other in terms of them, whether in co-operation or opposition. Dialectic may lead to discovering basic agreement and disagreement if it takes place in genuine dialogue, but not if it becomes a dialectical exercise within the mind of a single thinker. Such *ratio* is one of the things that distinguishes man from the animal, but it is not the decisive factor, as Plato thought. Nor is man understandable simply as the symbol-making animal, as Ernst Cassirer and Suzanne Langer hold. Basic to man as man is language, and language is, in the first instance, living speech between men.

Living speech presupposes the distancing which gives man the possibility of a world. It also presupposes the synthetic apperception whereby the world becomes one. But above all it presupposes that men become selves in relation with each other. Language is, in the first instance, neither the unmediated cry of the animal nor the universal Platonic idea, but the mediate–immediate dialogue between two persons, each of whom recognizes himself as a self when he is speaking to the other person and the other person as a self even when he is speaking to that person of himself. Our common world is, therefore, as Heracleitus points out, a cosmos built upon logos—the common speech-with-meaning. It is through this speech between man and man that we are confirmed as selves. It is through it too that we build up a world of language—of potential speech which again and again becomes actual in the spoken word. And it is through it, finally, that we build up a world of categories within which we think, communicate with one another, and develop our civilization. The true civilizing tool is not Prometheus' fire but speech.

Yet language remains curiously ambiguous—being born, dying, going over from lived speech to conventional phrase, from genuine dialogue to technical interchange, from inter-human contact to mass social manipulation. We must distinguish, therefore, between the word as direct dialogue, the word as category pointing back to the immediacy of lived speech, and the word which no longer points back but instead points out toward a world of technical interaction. It is this last word which leads toward the ultimate consummation of objectified, monological thought, the electronic brain, an invention which fits Descartes' definition of man as a 'thinking thing' as no human being ever has!

Useful as precision and definition are for the exact sciences, the true humanity and the very meaning of language depend upon its being brought back to the fruitful disagreement of lived speech between men whose meanings necessarily differ because of the difference of their attitudes, their situations, their points of view as persons.

11

'Guilt and Guilt Feelings', one of the longest essays in this book, is also one of the most important—as an extension of Buber's philosophical anthropology, as a base for his ethics, as a commentary on the culture of our times, and as an application of his thought to psychotherapy. The centrality of man's existence as We is basic to Buber's distinction in this essay between 'groundless' neurotic guilt—a subjective feeling within a person, usually unconscious and repressed, and 'existential' guilt—an ontic, interhuman reality in which the person dwells in the truest sense of the term. The analyst, writes Buber in the short precursor to this essay—'Healing through Meeting'— must see the illness of the patient as an illness of his relations with the world: 'A soul is never sick alone, but always through a betweenness, a situation between it and another existing being.' True guilt does not reside in the human person but in his failure to respond to the legitimate claim and address of the world. Similarly, the repression of guilt and the neuroses which result from this repression are not merely psychological phenomena but events between men.[1] Existential guilt, writes Buber in 'Guilt and Guilt Feelings', is 'guilt that a person has taken on himself as a person and in a personal situation'. Certainly there is purely social and even neurotic guilt derived from a set of mores and taboos imposed upon the individual by parents and society and incorporated into an internalized 'superego'. But there is also real guilt, guilt which has to do with one's actual stance in the world and the way in which one goes out from it to relate to other people. Real guilt is neither subjective nor objective. It is dialogical—the inseparable corollary of one's personal responsibility, one's answerability for authenticating one's own existence and, by the same token, for responding to the partners of one's existence, the other persons with whom one lives. Where there is personal responsibility, there must also be the possibility of real guilt—

[1] Buber, *Pointing the Way*, 'Healing through Meeting', pp. 95 ff.

37

guilt for failing to respond, for responding inadequately or too late, or without one's whole self. Such guilt is neither inner nor outer. One is not answerable for it either to oneself alone or to society apart from oneself, but to that very bond between oneself and others through which one again and again discovers the direction in which one can authenticate one's existence. If a relation with another cannot be reduced to what goes on within each of the two persons, then the guilt which one person has toward a partner in relationship cannot be reduced to the subjective guilt he feels. 'Existential guilt', writes Buber, 'occurs when someone injures an order of the human world whose foundations he knows and recognizes as those of his own existence and of all common human existence.' Hence existential guilt transcends the realm of inner feelings and of the self's relation to itself. But the order of the human world that one injures is not an objective absolute: it is the sphere of the 'interhuman' itself. This sphere and the guilt that arises in it cannot be identified with the taboos and restrictions of any particular culture and society. 'The depth of the guilt feeling is not seldom connected with just that part of the guilt that cannot be ascribed to the taboo-offence, hence with the existential guilt.'

Guilt is an essential factor in the person's relations to others: it performs the necessary function of leading him to desire to set these relations to rights. It is actually here, in the real guilt of the person who has not responded to the legitimate claim and address of the world, that the possibility of transformation and healing lies. The therapist may lead the man who suffers from existential guilt to the place where he himself can walk the road of illuminating that guilt, persevering in his identification of himself as the person who took on that guilt, and, in so far as his situation makes possible, restoring 'the order of being injured by him through the relation of an active devotion to the world'.

In Archibald MacLeish's play *J. B.*, J. B. demands of his 'comforters' that they show him his guilt. He is answered instead in generalities—by the Marxist who removes guilt into history, by the psychoanalyst who reduces it to the unconscious, by the priest who universalizes it in original sin. It

is Martin Buber's great merit that he has given us a philosophical ground for understanding guilt in its particular,
existential reality, that he takes guilt as seriously as he takes
the unique, unrepeatable person and the unique, unrepeatable
situations in which that person is addressed and must respond.
The full significance of Buber's contribution comes to light only
when we mark how much less concrete and particular are the
treatments of existential guilt by other existentialists. 'Original
guilt consists in remaining with oneself', writes Buber in
criticism of Martin Heidegger's concept of guilt. If the being
before whom this hour places one is not met with the truth of
one's whole life, then one is guilty.

> Heidegger is right to say that . . . we are able to discover a
> primal guilt. But we are not able to do this by isolating a part
> of life, the part where the existence is related to itself and to
> its own being, but by becoming aware of the whole life without
> reduction, the life in which the individual, in fact, is essentially
> related to something other than himself.[1]

Following Heidegger, the existential psychoanalyst Medard
Boss sees guilt as arising primarily from failing to fulfil one's
being and realize one's potentialities:

> If you lock up potentialities you are guilty against (or
> indebted to) what is given you in your origin, in your 'core'. In
> this existential condition of being indebted and being guilty
> are founded all guilt feelings, in whatever thousand and one
> concrete forms and malformations they may appear in actuality.[2]

One's potential uniqueness may be given, but the direction in
which one authenticates one's existence is not; one discovers
it in constantly renewed decisions in response to the demand
of concrete situations. When we are guilty, it is not because
we have failed to realize our potentialities, which we cannot

---

[1] *Between Man and Man,* 'What is Man?', pp. 165 f.
[2] Quoted in Rollo May, Ernest Angel, Henri F. Elienberger, eds., *Existence: A New Dimension in Psychiatry and Psychology* (New York: Basic Books, 1958), p. 53; (London: Mayflower, 1960).

know in the abstract, but because we have failed to bring the resources we find available to us at a given moment into our response to a particular situation that calls us out. This means that we cannot be guilty *a priori* to any ideal conception of the self, but only in relation to those moment-by-moment chances to authenticate our selves that come to us in the concrete situation. 'What is possible in a certain hour and what is impossible cannot be adequately ascertained by any foreknowledge', writes Buber in *Pointing the Way*. 'One does not learn the measure and limit of what is attainable in a desired direction otherwise than through going in this direction. The forces of the soul allow themselves to be measured only through one's using them.'[1] Our potentialities cannot be divorced from the discovery of our personal direction, and this comes not in the meeting of man with himself but with other men. The order of existence that one injures is one's own order as well as that of the others because it is the foundation and the very meaning of one's existence as self.

The denial of 'the depth of existential guilt beyond all mere violation of taboo' is what Freud sought to accomplish through relativizing guilt feeling genetically, says Buber. It is characteristic of that 'advanced' generation for which 'it now passes as proved . . . that no real guilt exists; only guilt-feeling and guilt convention'. This denial amounts to a crisis not only in the life of modern man but of man as such, for 'man is the being who is capable of becoming guilty and is capable of illuminating his guilt'.

12

'Man and His Image-Work' is Buber's anthropology of art. As such it represents the culmination of a long lifetime of active and informed interest in art, dating back to Buber's studies in the history of art and including discussions of art dispersed throughout sixty years of writing.

In 'Productivity and Existence', 1914 (*Pointing the Way*), Buber distinguishes between legitimate creativity and that specious productivity which wears itself out turning all experience into communication.

[1] *Pointing the Way*, 'Prophecy, Apocalyptic, and the Historical Hour', p. 206.

For the creative man this potentiality of form is a specific one, directed into the language of his particular art. If an intention is expressed in this direction, it is that of his genius, not that of a self-conscious resolution. The dynamic element of his experience does not affect its wholeness and purity. It is otherwise when in perceiving he already cherishes the deliberate intention of utilizing what he perceives. Then he disturbs the experience, stunts its growth, and taints the process of its becoming. Only the unarbitrary can grow properly and bear mature and healthy fruit. That man is legitimately creative who experiences so strongly and formatively that his experiences unite into an image that demands to be set forth, and who then works at his task with full consciousness of his art. But he who interferes with the spontaneity of perceiving, who does not allow the inner selection and formation to prevail, þut instead inserts an aim from the beginning, has forfeited the meaning of this perception, the meaning that lies above all aims.

Art is to be measured not by the aspirations of the artist, but by its intrinsic qualities. Yet 'in the inner circle those works alone count that have given form to the meaning of being'. 'The significance of an artist does not depend upon his morals'; yet there is an existential relationship between what the artist is and what he does. 'In inner development mastery and power accrue only to that artist who is worthy of his art.'[1]

Buber's philosophy of dialogue developed in close connection with his thought on art. His earliest positive mention of the I–Thou relationship is his 1905 article on the great actress Eleanora Duse. In 'With a Monist' (1914) the twofold relationship of man to what he meets that Buber later describes as I–Thou and I–It is expressed in terms of man's relation to the world of the senses.

There is an ordinary reality which suffices as a common denominator for the comparison and ordering of things. But the great reality is another. And how can I give this reality to my world except by . . . bending over the experienced thing

[1] *Pointing the Way*, pp. 8 ff.

41

with fervour and power and by melting the shell of passivity with the fire of my being until the confronting, the shaping, the bestowing side of things springs up to meet me and embraces me so that I know the world in it?

Through such experiencing of the bestowing side of things there appears to the true artist 'the secret shape of that thing which appeared to none before him'.[1]

In *I and Thou* (1923) Buber speaks of art as one of the forms of the I–Thou relationship. The 'ideal forms' that man meets as Thou are not Platonic archetypes but merely the potentialities of form that arise from man's meeting with the world:

This is the eternal source of art: a man is faced by a form which desires to be made through him into a work. This form is no offspring of his soul, but is an appearance which steps up to it and demands of it the effective power. . . . He who gives himself to it may withhold nothing of himself. . . . I can neither experience nor describe the form which meets me, but only body it forth. . . . To produce is to draw forth, to invent is to find, to shape is to discover.

Art exists as art only when the created form is taken up into the meeting of I and Thou and not when it is left as a detached object of observation and analysis. 'Form is disclosed to the artist as he looks at what is over against him. He banishes it to be a "structure".' The nature of this 'structure' is that it can be freed for a timeless moment by the meeting with the man who brings the form to life again in the presentness and immediacy of the I–Thou relationship.

In bodying forth I disclose. I lead the form across—into the world of *It*. The work produced is a thing among things, able to be experienced and described as a sum of qualities. But from time to time it can face the receptive beholder in its whole embodied form.[2]

---

[1] *Pointing the Way*, pp. 28 f.
[2] Martin Buber, *I and Thou*, pp. 9 f., 41 f.

A man may simply experience art: see it as qualities, analyse how it is made, and place it in the scheme of things. In this case it remains an It and its potentialities of ever new meeting remain unrealized. In art, as in life in general, the alternation between I–Thou and I–It is indispensable. Continuity of the I–Thou relationship is neither possible nor desirable. What is desirable is that the I–It relation serve as what it essentially is—the product of the I–Thou relationship which points back to it. The directness of the I–Thou relationship is established not only through the mediation of the senses, e.g., the concrete meeting of real living persons, but also through the mediation of the 'word', i.e., the mediation of those technical means and those fields of symbolic communication, such as language, music, art, and ritual, which enable men to enter into relation with what is over against them.

'All art is from its origin essentially of the nature of dialogue', writes Buber in 'Dialogue', 1929 (*Between Man and Man*).

All music calls to an ear not the musician's own, all sculpture to an eye not the sculptor's, architecture in addition calls to the step as it walks in the building. They all say to him who receives them, something (not a 'feeling' but a perceived mystery) that can be said only in this one language.

Artistic creation and appreciation, like the I–Thou relationship with nature, are modified forms of dialogue which by their very nature cannot be reciprocal. The artist, or 'onlooker' as Buber calls him in 'Dialogue', is not intent on analysing and noting traits, as is the observer, but instead sees the object freely 'and undisturbed awaits what will be presented to him'. He perceives an existence instead of a sum of traits, and he makes a genuine response to this existence.[1] This response manifests itself as creation of form rather than as answering with one's personal existence what addresses one. Yet it retains the betweenness, the presentness, and the uniqueness which characterize the true I–Thou relationship as distinct from I–It.

'Each great painter is a discoverer', writes Buber in his

[1] Martin Buber, *Between Man and Man*, pp. 8 ff., 25.

43

critique of 'Bergson's Concept of Intuition', 1943 (*Pointing the Way*).

But he is just the discoverer of an 'aspect'; that is, of a view of the world in which a certain manner of seeing manifests itself that is peculiar to him, this painter. This aspect is, of course, something that would not have become visible unless his eyes had beheld it.

Perception, Buber adds, cannot be divorced from our active relation to what we perceive if we are to understand the origin of art. 'The decisive event that engenders the work of art is not the perception of a being but the vital contact with the being, an ever-renewed vital contact . . . in which the experience of the senses only fits in as a factor.' This contact is not itself displayed in the work, but powers are put in motion by it through whose transformation the work arises. 'The artist does not hold a fragment of being up to the light; he perceives from his contact with being and brings forth what has never before existed.'[1]

'Man and His Image-Work' elaborates Buber's understanding of art as dialogue, but it does so on the additional basis of the anthropological groundwork that Buber has laid in 'Distance and Relation' (1951). It is not enough for man to use and possess things. He also has a great desire to enter into personal relation with things and to imprint on them his relation to them, and this is the first step toward the creation of art. 'Art is neither the impression of natural objectivity nor the expression of spiritual subjectivity', writes Buber, rejecting the two alternatives with which we are most familiar in aesthetics. It is the realm of 'the between' that has become form—the witness of the relation between the human substance and the substance of things. The great nude sculpture of the ages cannot be understood 'either from the givenness of the human body or from the will to expression of an inner state, but solely from the relational event which takes place between two entities which have gone apart from one another'.

In 'Man and His Image-Work' Buber asks what art tells

---

[1] *Pointing the Way*, p. 84.

us about man as man. Free as the artist may hold himself from nature, his work is still bound to the life of the senses and to his meeting with the world. To Kant's statement that we can only know of the 'thing in itself' that it is, Buber adds for modern man the assertion 'and that the existent meets us'. This is a powerful knowing, Buber claims, 'for in all the world of the senses there is not one trait that does not stem from meetings, that does not originate in the co-working of the x in the meeting'.

'Man and His Image-Work' represents a significant development in Buber's theory of knowledge. This theory of knowledge points to the I–Thou relationship as an entirely other way of knowing, yet one from which the I–It, or subject–object, relation is derived. Buber agrees with Kant that we cannot know any object in itself apart from its relation to a knowing subject. At the same time, through the presentness and concreteness of the meeting with the 'other', Buber avoids the pitfalls of Descartes, who abstracts the subject into isolated consciousness; of the idealist, who removes reality into the knowing subject; and of Kant himself, who asserts that we cannot know reality, but only the categories of our thought.[1] Taken together 'Distance and Relation' and 'Man and His Image-Work' are the most explicit and sustained treatment of epistemology in Buber's writings. Our relation to nature is founded on numberless connections between movements to something and perceptions of something, says Buber, following the psychology of Viktor von Weizsaecker and Erwin Straus.[2] Even the images of fantasy draw their material from this foundation. That to which we move and which we perceive is always sensible. The sense world itself arises out of the intercourse of being and being.

On the basis of this theory of knowledge Buber constructs his aesthetic. All men deepen perception into vision through 'figurating', but only the artist is 'full of figure'. The sense

---

[1] For a fullscale discussion of Buber's epistemology see Maurice Friedman, *Martin Buber: The Life of Dialogue* (New York: Harper & Row, 1960; London: Routledge, 1955), chap. 19.

[2] Viktor von Weizsaecker, *Der Gestaltkreis, Theorie der Einheit von Wahrnehmen und Bewegungen* (3rd ed.; Stuttgart: Georg Thieme Verlag, 1947); Erwin Straus, *Vom Sinn der Sinne*; published in English under the title *The Primary World*, trans. by Jacob Needleman (New York: The Free Press, 1963; London: Collier-Macmillan, 1964).

world is a preliminary stage on the way to this artistic vision' and 'vision is figurating faithfulness to the unknown and does its work in co-operation with it'. The meeting of artist and world is not an encounter between perception and sense-object, but between the being of the artist and the being of the x. In art, as in knowledge, love, and faith—the other three potencies by which the human transcends the natural—dissatisfaction with being limited to needs and longing for perfect relation, raise man's meeting with the world to a higher and fuller dimension. The artist fashions the sense world anew through his figuration in vision and in work—not through trying to penetrate behind the world of the senses, but through completing its form to the perfect work of figuration.

Martin Buber has grounded art in man's basic relation to other being as no other thinker has done, says Louis Hammer, in comment on 'Man and His Image-Work'. What is more, he has steered clear of the equally unsatisfying alternatives of labelling art cognitive or relegating it to 'mere emotion' or to the production of 'valuable attitudes'. For Buber, the work of art is not, as it is for Suzanne Langer, a virtual image reflecting a pattern of feeling. 'It is figuration, encountered and discovered in the world, and brought to full actualization.' By seeing art as a basic capacity for meeting the world rather than as merely a matter of symbolic function, Buber goes beyond the view of art as representational. 'The world is not represented in art—it is allowed to take on concrete form within the range of one of the senses or of language. . . . It is not the likeness to common-sense objects or the lack of such likeness which makes a painting good or bad. It is faithfulness to emergent form, the development given to visual figuration, that makes the difference.'

The symbolic view sees art as giving form to feeling and as ordering emotional life, but it neglects the relation between the person and the world and thus 'leaves the way open for the abandonment of the world that characterizes contemporary painting', for the retreat 'into a private realm in which the spatially "interesting" or "impressive" or "shocking" holds full sway'. In opposition to this tendency, and in close consonance with that existential trust which stands at the core of

Buber's 'life of dialogue', Hammer suggests that the genuine centre of art is found where some reconciliation between the artist and the external world occurs, 'where some measure of trust is established, so that the artist does not run away from the world, but stands his ground'.

The artistic imagination leads the person to the world that has been set at a distance and enables him to retrieve that world. The artist necessarily distorts or abstracts from common-sense objects in their everyday appearance. But, in his genuine moments, he does so to win back the world in its relevance to man. He celebrates the range and variety of forms accessible to man within the sense world.

Hammer also contrasts Buber's view with R. G. Collingwood's expressionist theory of art, according to which the artist struggles with the hiddenness of feeling within his own psyche in order to attain a clear individual presentation of emotional experience. Such emotional clarification may be a by-product, Hammer points out, but it cannot be the goal. Emotion is not separable 'from the lineaments of the Other rendered accessible through sensible qualities. . . . Emotion is a felt pattern in our awareness of ourselves in relation to what surrounds us.' Through the elaboration of figuration the artist attains Collingwood's goal of making emotion definite and clear, but his focus is on the figuration and not the emotion. By the same token art cannot be reduced to Kierkegaard's 'aesthetic' category in which one seeks what is interesting to escape from boredom. Art is not an alternative to the ethical or religious life, as Kierkegaard thought, for it too takes place in wholeness, the wholeness of the artist who says 'Thou' to what meets him in the sense world.

The genuine artist, at the centre . . . lives in the tension found everywhere within the life of dialogue. He must live and move within the limited, finite, appearing human world, and through his inner faithfulness endeavor to participate in the redemption of that world, creating as he can a work that 'interests' and 'moves' because it speaks with the power of what is in being.

Buber's understanding of the aesthetic follows the test of his philosophy in avoiding the alternatives of the objective and the subjective in favour of the 'narrow ridge'—'the between' where the person meets what is in the world.[1] Traditional accounts, writes Hammer, 'have tended to consider beauty a quality which an object possesses, whether through the supervenience of a transcendental form or as the result of a complex of natural qualities'. In contrast to this view are those subjectivists who see beauty as in the eye, or the experience of the beholder, such as Santayana's 'pleasure objectified'.[2] From the point of view of Buber's 'Man and His Image-Work', in contrast, 'beauty is not some emergent quality of objects or an affective state', but the product of our dialogue with sensible being. What beauty is in itself, however, Buber does not tell us. 'I am inclined', Buber writes me, 'to think beauty a mystery that we should not try to define.'[3]

13

What Buber says in 'Man and His Image-Work' of the ontological significance of all philosophical anthropology is especially true of his own:

Every anthropology of a subject touches on its ontology, hence every investigation of a subject in its conditioning by the manner, the nature, the attitude of man leads us toward this subject's place in being and its function in meaning. Thus to the degree that we fathom the relation of a circle of reality to us, we are always referred to its still unfathomed relation to being and meaning.

Martin Buber's philosophical anthropology refers us with a profundity unequalled in our time to man's still unfathomed relation to being and meaning.

[1] Cf. Maurice Friedman, *Martin Buber: The Life of Dialogue*, chap. 1.
[2] Louis Z. Hammer, 'The Relevance of Buber's Thought to Aesthetics', *The Philosophy of Martin Buber*, loc. cit.
[3] Letter from Martin Buber to Maurice Friedman, Feb. 19, 1963.

CHAPTER II

DISTANCE AND RELATION[1]

1

The question I wish to raise is that of the principle of human life, that is, its beginning.

This cannot be thought of here as a beginning in time. It is not sensible to try to discover when and how a certain species of life, instead of being content like the rest with the perception of things and conditions, began to perceive its own perceiving as well. The only way is to consider, in all its paradox and actuality, the category of being characterized by the name of man, in order to experience its ground and its beginning.

It would be quite wrong to make the reality of the spirit the starting point of the question. The one way to expose the principle of a being is first to contrast its reality with that of other known beings. But the reality of the spirit is not given to us apart from man: all the spiritual life which is given to us has its reality in him. Nature alone presents itself to us for this act of contrasting—nature which certainly includes man but which, as soon as we penetrate to his essentiality, is compelled to loosen its grasp and even to relinquish for our separate consideration this child which from its standpoint is an aberration. This separate consideration takes place thereafter not within nature, but starts from nature.

Starting from nature, that is, in this case, starting from the association of 'living beings' to which man, so far as he is a part of nature, must be reckoned as belonging—does not mean noting those characteristics which distinguish him from the

[1] Trans. by Ronald Gregor Smith.

49

others, but it means examining the ground of being of those characteristics as a whole. Only in this way shall we learn both the fact and the reason for the fact that those distinguishing characteristics as a whole constitute not only a special group of beings but a special way of being, and thus constitute a special category of being. The act of contrasting, carried out properly and adequately, leads to the grasp of the principle.

In this way we reach the insight that the principle of human life is not simple but twofold, being built up in a twofold movement which is of such kind that the one movement is the presupposition of the other. I propose to call the first movement 'the primal setting at a distance' and the second 'entering into relation'. That the first movement is the presupposition of the other is plain from the fact that one can enter into relation only with being which has been set at a distance, more precisely, has become an independent opposite. And it is only for man that an independent opposite exists.

The double principle cannot be demonstrated in the first instance in man's 'inner life', but in the great phenomena of his connection with an otherness which is constituted as otherness by the event of 'distancing'. When the principle has been demonstrated in this way its working out in the inner life of the human person will become clear.

Modern biology speaks of an animal's environment (*Umwelt*), by which is understood the total world of objects accessible to its senses, as conditioned by the circumstances of life which are peculiar to this animal. An animal—something of this kind is said—perceives only the things which concern it in the total situation available to it, and it is those things which make its world (*Umwelt*). But it seems questionable whether the concept of a world is rightly used here, whether we are justified in regarding the context described as an environment as a kind of world, and not simply as a kind of realm. For by 'world' we must mean that which is extended substantially beyond the realm of the observer who is *in* the world and as such is independent. Even a 'world of the senses' is a world through being composed not of sense data alone, but through what is perceived being completed by what can be perceived, and it is the unity of these two which constitutes the proper 'world' of the senses. An animal's organism gathers, continuously or continually, the elements which meet the necessities and wants of its life, in order to construct from them the circle of its existence. Wherever swallows or tunny wander, their bodily being (*Leiblichkeit*) carries out this selection from 'nature', which as such is completely unknown to them, and on which they in turn have an effect, again as on something which they neither know nor can know. An animal's 'image of the world', or rather, its image of a realm, is nothing more than the dynamic of the presences bound up with one another by bodily memory to the extent required by the functions of life which are to be carried out. This image depends on, it clings to, the animal's activities.

It is only man who replaces this unsteady conglomeration, whose constitution is suited to the lifetime of the individual organism, by a unity which can be imagined or thought by him as existing for itself. With soaring power he reaches out beyond what is given him, flies beyond the horizon and the familiar stars, and grasps a totality. With him, with his human life, a world exists. The meeting of natural being with the living creature produces those more or less changing masses of usable sense data which constitute the animal's realm of life. But only from the meeting of natural being with man does the new and enduring arise, that which comprehends and infinitely transcends the realm. An animal in the realm of its perceptions is like a fruit in its skin; man is, or can be, in the world as a dweller in an enormous building which is always being added to, and to whose limits he can never penetrate, but which he can nevertheless know as one does know a house in which one lives—for he is capable of grasping the wholeness of the building as such. Man is like this because he is the creature (*Wesen*) through whose being (*Sein*) 'what is' (*das Seiende*) becomes detached from him, and recognized for itself. It is only the realm which is removed, lifted out from sheer presence, withdrawn from the operation of needs and wants, set at a distance and thereby given over to itself, which is more and other than a realm. Only when a structure of being is independently over against a living being (*Seiende*), an independent opposite, does a world exist.

51

The view could be put forward that this giving of independence to a world is the result of agelong developments of mankind, and that it can therefore not be constitutive of man as such. But it cannot concern us when and how the category of man has been realized; our concern is its ground. When a world exists, and to the extent to which it exists, there exists the man who conditions it, and he is there not in the sense of a species of living creatures, but of a category which has moved into reality. No matter where you meet man on his way, he always holds over against himself to some degree, in some way, that which he does not know as well as that which he knows, bound up together in one world, however 'primitive'. This is of course true of his connection with time no less than of his connection with space. An animal's actions are concerned with its future and the future of its young, but only man imagines the future: the beaver's dam is extended in a time-realm, but the planted tree is rooted in the world of time, and he who plants the first tree is he who will expect the Messiah.

Now the second movement has been added to the first: Man turns to the withdrawn structure of being (*Seiende*) and enters into relation with it. 'First' and 'second' are not to be taken in the sense of a temporal succession; it is not possible to think of an existence over against a world which is not also an attitude to it as a world, and that means the outline of an attitude of relation. This is to say no more than that an animal does not know the state of relation because one cannot stand in a relation to something that is not perceived as contrasted and existing for itself. The rainmaker who deals with the cloud that is sailing up beyond the orbit of his sight acts within the same category as the physicist who has worked out the existence of the still unseen planet, and communicates with it at his desk.

We may characterize the act and the work of entering into relation with the world as such—and, therefore, not with parts of it, and not with the sum of its parts, but with it as the world —as synthesizing apperception, by which we establish that this pregnant use of the concept involves the function of unity: by synthesizing apperception I mean the apperception of a being as a whole and as a unity. Such a view is won, and won again and again, only by looking upon the world as a world. The

52

conception of wholeness and unity is in its origin identical with the conception of the world to which man is turned. He who turns to the realm which he has removed from himself, and which has been completed and transformed into a world—he who turns to the world and looking upon it steps into relation with it, becomes aware of wholeness and unity in such a way that from then on he is able to grasp being as a wholeness and a unity; the single being has received the character of wholeness and the unity which are perceived in it from the wholeness and unity perceived in the world. But a man does not obtain this view simply from the 'setting at a distance' and 'making independent'. These would offer him the world only as an object, as which it is only an aggregate of qualities that can be added to at will, not a genuine wholeness and unity. Only the view of what is over against me in the world in its full presence, with which I have set myself, present in my whole person, in relation—only this view gives me the world truly as whole and one. For only in such an opposition are the realm of man and what completes it in spirit, finally one. So it has always been, and so it is in this hour.

What has been indicated here must not be misunderstood as meaning that I 'establish' the world, or the like. Man's act of setting at a distance is no more to be understood as primary than his act of relation which is bound up with it. Rather is this the peculiarity of human life, that here and here alone a being has arisen from the whole, endowed and entitled to detach the whole as a world from himself and to make it an opposite to himself, instead of cutting out with his senses the part he needs from it, as all other beings do, and being content with that. This endowment and this entitlement of man produce, out of the whole, the being of the world, and this being can only mean that it is there for man as something that is for itself, with which he is able to enter into relation.

We must now look afresh at the twofold nature of the principle. Though the two movements are bound together in it very closely and with many strands, yet they are not to be understood as just two aspects of the same event or process. There is no kind of parallelism here, nothing that would make the carrying out of the one movement bring about the carrying out of the other. Rather it must be firmly maintained that the first creates the presupposition for the second—not its source, but its presupposition. With the appearance of the first, therefore, nothing more than room for the second is given. It is only at this point that the real history of the spirit begins, and this history takes its eternal rise in the extent to which the second movement shares in the intimations of the first, to the extent of their mutual interaction, reaction, and co-operation. Man can set at a distance without coming into real relation with what has been set at a distance. He can fill the act of setting at a distance with the will to relation, relation having been made possible only by that act; he can accomplish the act of relation in the acknowledgment of the fundamental actuality of the distance. But the two movements can also contend with one another, each seeing in the other the obstacle to its own realization. And finally, in moments and forms of grace, unity can arise from the extreme tension of the contradiction as the overcoming of it, which is granted only now and in this way.

2

He who, with his eyes on the twofold principle of human life, attempts to trace the spirit's course in history, must note that the great phenomena on the side of acts of distance are preponderantly universal, and those on the side of acts of relation preponderantly personal, as indeed corresponds to their connection with one another. The facts of the movement of distance yield the essential answer to the question, How is man possible; the facts of the movement of relation yield the essential answer to the question, How is human life realized. The first question is strictly one about category; the second is one of category and history. Distance provides the human situation; relation provides man's becoming in that situation.

This difference can be seen in two spheres, within the connection with things and within the connection with one's fellow men.

An animal also makes use of things. In fact it is in animals that we can observe using in the exact sense, when they turn something, on which they happen, round and round until they reach the possibility of using it for the attainment of a definite purpose, whether preconceived or arising at that moment. Monkeys make use of a stick they have found in order to force an opening which they could not have made with the arm, they make use of a stone to crack nuts. But they do not set aside any of these things, which for the moment have become tools, in order to use them the next day in a similar fashion; clearly none of them persists in their consciousness as a thing in which the faculty of the lever or the hammer dwells. These things are to hand, as occasion arises, in their realm; they never receive their place in a world. Only man, as man, gives distance to things which he comes upon in his realm; he sets them in their independence as things which from now on continue to exist ready for a function and which he can make wait for him so that on each occasion he may master them again, and bring them into action. A suitable piece of metal which has once been used as an auger does not cease to be an auger: it persists in the quality which has now been made known, this very piece of metal, this specific It with its known capacity now persists there; it is at one's disposal. Every change made in the stuff of things which is intended to make them more suitable for fulfilling a purpose, every strengthening and refining, every differentiation and combination, every technique is built on this elementary basis—that a person sets aside something which he finds, and makes it into something for itself, in which state, however, having become a tool, it can always be found again, and always as this same tool ready to carry out this same work. A monkey can swing the branch of a tree as a weapon; but man alone is capable of providing the branch with a separate existence, in that it is thenceforth established as a 'weapon' and awaits man's pleasure to be used again. Whatever is done to it after that to shape it into a proper cudgel, there is no further essential change: technique only fulfils what has been given by the primary choice and assignment, by a primary nomos.

But now something new and essentially different can enter the situation.

Let us think of a tribe which is close to nature, and which already knows the axe, a simple but reliable stone-axe. Then it occurs to a lad to scratch a curved line on his axe with the aid of a sharper stone. This is a picture of something and of nothing: it may be a sign, but even its author does not know of what. What was in his mind? Magic—to give the tool a more powerful effect? Or simply a play with the possibility presented by the empty space on the shaft? The two things are not mutually exclusive, but they mingle—the magical intention concentrates the play in more solid forms, the free play loosens the form decided on by magic and changes it—but even together these do not suffice to explain the unheard-of fact that a work has been carried out without any model, reaching beyond the technical purpose. We have to turn to the principle of human life in its twofold character in order to establish what has happened. Man sets things which he uses at a distance, he gives them into an independence in which function gains duration, he reduces and empowers them to be the bearers of the function. In this way the first movement of the principle is satisfied, but the second is not. Man has a great desire to enter into personal relation with things and to imprint on them his relation to them. To use them, even to possess them, is not enough, they must become his in another way, by imparting to them in the picture-sign his relation to them.

But the picture-sign grows to be a picture; it ceases to be accessory to a tool and becomes an independent structure. The form indicated by even the clumsiest ornament is now fulfilled in an autonomous region as the sediment of man's relation to things. Art is neither the impression of natural objectivity nor the expression of spiritual subjectivity, but it is the work and witness of the relation between the *substantia humana* and the *substantia rerum*, it is the realm of 'the between' which has become a form. Consider great nude sculptures of the ages: None of them is to be understood properly either from the giveness of the human body or from the will to expression of an inner state, but solely from the relational event which takes place between two entities which have gone apart from one another, the withdrawn 'body' and the withdrawing 'soul'. In each of the arts there is something specifically corresponding to the relational character to be found in the picture. Music, for example, can be understood in terms of categories only

56

when it is recognized that music is the ever renewed discovering of tonal being in the movement of 'distancing' and the releasing of this tonal being in the movement of relation by bodying it forth.

3

The twofold principle of human life can be still more fully clarified in men's relation to one another.

In an insect state the system of division of labour excludes not merely every variation, but also every granting of a function in the precise sense of an individual award. In human society at all its levels persons confirm one another in a practical way to some extent or other in their personal qualities and capacities, and a society may be termed human in the measure to which its members confirm one another. Apart from the technique of the tool and from the weapon, what has enabled this creature, so badly equipped 'by nature', to assert himself and to achieve lordship of the earth is this dynamic, adaptable, pluralistic form of association, which has been made possible by the factor of mutual individual completion of function and the corresponding factor of mutual individual recognition of function. Within the most closely bound clan there still exist free societies of fishers, free orders of barter, free associations of many kinds, which are built upon acknowledged differences in capacity and inclination. In the most rigid epochs of ancient kingdoms the family preserved its separate structure, in which, despite its authoritative quality, individuals affirmed one another in their manifold nature. And everywhere the position of society is strengthened by this balance of firmness and looseness. Man has always stood opposed to natural powers as the creature equipped with the tool which awaits him in independence, who forms his associations of independent single lives. An animal never succeeds in unravelling its companions from the knot of their common life, just as it never succeeds in ascribing to the enemy an existence beyond his hostility, that is, beyond its own realm. Man, as man, sets man at a distance and makes him independent; he lets the life of men like himself go on round about him, and so he, and he alone, is able to enter into relation, in his own individual status, with those like himself. The basis of man's life with man is twofold, and it is one—the wish of every man to be confirmed as what he is, even as what he can become, by men; and the innate capacity in man to confirm his fellow men in this way. That this capacity lies so immeasurably fallow constitutes the real weakness and questionableness of the human race: actual humanity exists only where this capacity unfolds. On the other hand, of course, an empty claim for confirmation, without devotion for being and becoming, again and again mars the truth of the life between man and man.

The great characteristic of men's life with one another, speech, is doubly significant as a witness to the principle of human life. Men express themselves to men in a way that is different, not in kind or degree but essentially, from the way animals express themselves to their companions. Man and many animals have this is common, that they call out to others; to speak to others is something essentially human, and is based on the establishment and acknowledgment of the independent otherness of the other with whom one fosters relation, addressing and being addressed on this very basis.[1] The oldest form of word, along with—and perhaps even before—the 'holophrastic' characterization of situations by means of words in the form of sentences, which signified the situations for those who had to be informed, may have been the individual's name: when the name let the companion and helper at a distance know that his presence, his and none other, was needed in a given situation. Both the holophrase and the name are still signals, yet also words; for—and this is the second part of the witness of speech to the principle of human life—man sets also his calls at a distance and gives them independence, he stores them, like a tool he has prepared, as objects which are ready for use, he makes them into words which exist by themselves. Here in speech the addressing of another as it were cancels out, it is neutralized—but in order to come again and again to life, not indeed in those popular discussions which misuse the reality

[1] Animals, especially domestic animals, are capable of regarding a man in a 'speaking' way; they turn to him as one to whom they wish to announce themselves, but not as a being existing for himself as well, outside this addressing of him. On this remarkable frontier area, cf. Buber, *I and Thou*, pp. 96 ff., 125 f., and *Between Man and Man*, p. 22 f.

of speech, but in genuine conversation. If we ever reach the stage of making ourselves understood only by means of the dictograph, that is, without contact with one another, the chance of human growth would be indefinitely lost.

Genuine conversation, and therefore every actual fulfilment of relation between men, means acceptance of otherness. When two men inform one another of their basically different views about an object, each aiming to convince the other of the rightness of his own way of looking at the matter, everything depends so far as human life is concerned, on whether each thinks of the other as the one he is, whether each, that is, with all his desire to influence the other, nevertheless unreservedly accepts and confirms him in his being this man and in his being made in this particular way. The strictness and depth of human individuation, the elemental otherness of the other, is then not merely noted as the necessary starting point, but is affirmed from the one being to the other. The desire to influence the other then does not mean the effort to change the other, to inject one's own 'rightness' into him; but it means the effort to let that which is recognized as right, as just, as true (and for that very reason must also be established there, in the substance of the other) through one's influence take seed and grow in the form suited to individuation. Opposed to this effort is the lust to make use of men by which the manipulator of 'propaganda' and 'suggestion' is possessed, in his relation to men remaining as in a relation to things, to things, moreover, with which he will never enter into relation, which he is indeed eager to rob of their distance and independence.

Human life and humanity come into being in genuine meetings. There man learns not merely that he is limited by man, cast upon his own finitude, partialness, need of completion, but his own relation to truth is heightened by the other's different relation to the same truth—different in accordance with his individuation, and destined to take seed and grow differently. Men need, and it is granted to them, to confirm one another in their individual being by means of genuine meetings. But beyond this they need, and it is granted to them, to see the truth, which the soul gains by its struggle, light up to the others, the brothers, in a different way, and even so be confirmed.

4

The realization of the principle in the sphere between men reaches its height in an event which may be called 'making present'. As a partial happening something of this is to be found wherever men come together, but in its essential formation I should say it appears only rarely. It rests on a capacity possessed to some extent by everyone, which may be described as 'imagining' the real: I mean the capacity to hold before one's soul a reality arising at this moment but not able to be directly experienced. Applied to intercourse between men, 'imagining' the real means that I imagine to myself what another man is at this very moment wishing, feeling, perceiving, thinking, and not as a detached content but in his very reality, that is, as a living process in this man. The full 'making present' surpasses this in one decisive way: something of the character of what is imagined is joined to the act of imagining, that is, something of the character of an act of the will is added to my imagining of the other's act of will, and so on. So-called fellow feeling may serve as a familiar illustration of this if we leave vague sympathy out of consideration and limit the concept to that event in which I experience, let us say, the specific pain of another in such a way that I feel what is specific in it, not, therefore, a general discomfort or state of suffering, but this particular pain as the pain of the other. This making present increases until it is a paradox in the soul when I and the other are embraced by a common living situation, and (let us say) the pain which I inflict upon him surges up in myself, revealing the abyss of the contradictoriness of life between man and man. At such a moment something can come into being which cannot be built up in any other way.

The principle of human life which we have recognized suggests how making present may be understood in its ontological significance. Within the setting of the world at a distance and the making it independent, yet also essentially reaching beyond this and in the proper sense not able to be included in it, is the fact of man's himself being set at a distance and made independent as 'the others'. Our fellow men, it is true, live round about us as components of the independent world over against us, but in so far as we grasp each one as a human being he ceases to be a component and is there in his self-being as I am; his being at a distance does not exist merely for me, but it cannot be separated from the fact of my being at a distance for him. The first movement of human life puts men into mutual existence which is fundamental and even. But the second movement puts them into mutual relation with me which happens from time to time and by no means in an even way, but depends on our carrying it out. Relation is fulfilled in a full making present when I think of the other not merely as this very one, but experience, in the particular approximation of the given moment, the experience belonging to him as this very one. Here and now for the first time does the other become a self for me, and the making independent of his being which was carried out in the first movement of distancing is shown in a new highly pregnant sense as a presupposition—a presupposition of this 'becoming a self for me', which is, however, to be understood not in a psychological but in a strictly ontological sense, and should therefore rather be called 'becoming a self with me'. But it is ontologically complete only when the other knows that he is made present by me in his self and when this knowledge induces the process of his inmost self-becoming. For the inmost growth of the self is not accomplished, as people like to suppose today, in man's relation to himself, but in the relation between the one and the other, between men, that is, pre-eminently in the mutuality of the making present—in the making present of another self and in the knowledge that one is made present in his own self by the other—together with the mutuality of acceptance, of affirmation and confirmation.

Man wishes to be confirmed in his being by man, and wishes to have a presence in the being of the other. The human person needs confirmation because man as man needs it. An animal does not need to be confirmed, for it is what it is unquestionably. It is different with man: Sent forth from the natural domain of species into the hazard of the solitary category, surrounded by the air of a chaos which came into being with him, secretly and bashfully he watches for a Yes which allows him to be and which can come to him only from one human person to another. It is from one man to another that the heavenly bread of self-being is passed.

61

CHAPTER III

ELEMENTS OF THE INTERHUMAN[1]

THE SOCIAL AND THE INTERHUMAN

It is usual to ascribe what takes place between men to the social realm, thereby blurring a basically important line of division between two essentially different areas of human life. I myself, when I began nearly fifty years ago to find my own bearings in the knowledge of society, making use of the then unknown concept of the interhuman,[2] made the same error. From that time it became increasingly clear to me that we have to do here with a separate category of our. existence, even a separate dimension, to use a mathematical term, and one with which we are so familiar that its peculiarity has hitherto almost escaped us. Yet insight into its peculiarity is extremely important not only for our thinking, but also for our living.

We may speak of social phenomena wherever the life of a number of men, lived with one another, bound up together, brings in its train shared experiences and reactions. But to be thus bound up together means only that each individual existence is enclosed and contained in a group existence. It does not mean that between one member and another of the group there exists any kind of personal relation. They do feel that they belong together in a way that is, so to speak, fundamentally different from every possible belonging together with someone

[1] Trans. by Ronald Gregor Smith.

[2] 'Das Zwischenmenschliche.' See my Introduction to Werner Sombart, *Das Proletariat*, Vol. 1 in *Die Gesellschaft: Sammlung sozialpsychologischer Monographien*, ed. by Martin Buber (1st ed.; Frankfurt am Main: Rütten & Loening 1906).

outside the group. And there do arise, especially in the life of smaller groups, contacts which frequently favour the birth of individual relations, but, on the other hand, frequently make it more difficult. In no case, however, does membership in a group necessarily involve an existential relation between one member and another. It is true that there have been groups in history which included highly intensive and intimate relations between two of their members—as, for instance, in the homosexual relations among the Japanese Samurai or among Doric warriors —and these were countenanced for the sake of the stricter cohesion of the group. But in general it must be said that the leading elements in groups, especially in the later course of human history, have rather been inclined to suppress the personal relation in favour of the purely collective element. Where this latter element reigns alone or is predominant, men feel themselves to be carried by the collectivity, which lifts them out of loneliness and fear of the world and lostness. When this happens—and for modern man it is an essential happening —the life between person and person seems to retreat more and more before the advance of the collective. The collective aims at holding in check the inclination to personal life. It is as though those who are bound together in groups should in the main be concerned only with the work of the group and should turn to the personal partners, who are tolerated by the group, only in secondary meetings.

The difference between the two realms became very palpable to me on one occasion when I had joined the procession through a large town of a movement to which I did not belong. I did it out of sympathy for the tragic development which I sensed was at hand in the destiny of a friend who was one of the leaders of the movement. While the procession was forming, I conversed with him and with another, a goodhearted 'wild man', who also had the mark of death upon him. At that moment I still felt that the two men really were there, over against me, each of them a man near to me, near even in what was most remote from me; so different from me that my soul continually suffered from this difference, yet by virtue of this very difference confronting me with authentic being. Then the formations started off, and after a short time I was lifted out of all confrontation, drawn into the procession, falling in with its aimless step; and it was obviously the very same for the two with whom I had just exchanged human words. After a while we passed a café where I had been sitting the previous day with a musician whom I knew only slightly. The very moment we passed it the door opened, the musician stood on the threshold, saw me, apparently saw me alone, and waved to me. Straightway it seemed to me as though I were taken out of the procession and of the presence of my marching friends, and set there, confronting the musician. I forgot that I was walking along with the same step; I felt that I was standing over there by the man who had called out to me, and without a word, with a smile of understanding, was answering him. When consciousness of the facts returned to me, the procession, with my companions and myself at its head, had left the café behind.

The realm of the interhuman goes far beyond that of sympathy. Such simple happenings can be part of it as, for instance, when two strangers exchange glances in a crowded streetcar, at once to sink back again into the convenient state of wishing to know nothing about each other. But also every casual encounter between opponents belongs to this realm, when it affects the opponent's attitude—that is, when something, however imperceptible, happens between the two, no matter whether it is marked at the time by any feeling or not. The only thing that matters is that for each of the two men the other happens as the particular other, that each becomes aware of the other and is thus related to him in such a way that he does not regard and use him as his object, but as his partner in a living event, even if it is no more than a boxing match. It is well known that some existentialists assert that the basic factor between men is that one is an object for the other. But so far as this is actually the case, the special reality of the interhuman, the fact of the contact, has been largely eliminated. It cannot indeed be entirely eliminated. As a crude example, take two men who are observing one another. The essential thing is not that the one makes the other his object, but the fact that he is not fully able to do so and the reason for his failure. We have in common with all existing beings that we can be made objects of observation. But it is my privilege as man that by the hidden activity of my being I can establish an impassable barrier to objectification. Only in partnership can my being be perceived as an existing whole.

The sociologist may object to any separation of the social and the interhuman on the ground that society is actually built upon human relations, and the theory of these relations is therefore to be regarded as the very foundation of sociology. But here an ambiguity in the concept 'relation' becomes evident. We speak, for instance, of a comradely relation between two men in their work, and do not merely mean what happens between them as comrades, but also a lasting disposition which is actualized in those happenings and which even includes purely psychological events such as the recollection of the absent comrade. But by the sphere of the interhuman I mean solely actual happenings between men, whether wholly mutual or tending to grow into mutual relations. For the participation of both partners is in principle indispensable. The sphere of the interhuman is one in which a person is confronted by the other. We call its unfolding the dialogical.

In accordance with this, it is basically erroneous to try to understand the interhuman phenomena as psychological. When two men converse together, the psychological is certainly an important part of the situation, as each listens and each prepares to speak. Yet this is only the hidden accompaniment to the conversation itself, the phonetic event fraught with meaning, whose meaning is to be found neither in one of the two partners nor in both together, but only in their dialogue itself, in this 'between' which they live together.

BEING AND SEEMING

The essential problem of the sphere of the interhuman is the duality of being and seeming.

Although it is a familiar fact that men are often troubled about the impression they make on others, this has been much more discussed in moral philosophy than in anthropology. Yet this is one of the most important subjects for anthropological study.

We may distinguish between two different types of human

existence. The one proceeds from what one really is, the other from what one wishes to seem. In general, the two are found mixed together. There have probably been few men who were entirely independent of the impression they made on others, while there has scarcely existed one who was exclusively determined by the impression made by him. We must be content to distinguish between men in whose essential attitude the one or the other predominates.

This distinction is most powerfully at work, as its nature indicates, in the interhuman realm—that is, in men's personal dealings with one another.

Take as the simplest and yet quite clear example the situation in which two persons look at one another—the first belonging to the first type, the second to the second. The one who lives from his being looks at the other just as one looks at someone with whom he has personal dealings. His look is 'spontaneous', 'without reserve'; of course he is not uninfluenced by the desire to make himself understood by the other, but he is uninfluenced by any thought of the idea of himself which he can or should awaken in the person whom he is looking at. His opposite is different. Since he is concerned with the image which his appearance, and especially his look or glance, produces in the other, he 'makes' this look. With the help of the capacity, in greater or lesser degree peculiar to man, to make a definite element of his being appear in his look, he produces a look which is meant to have, and often enough does have, the effect of a spontaneous utterance—not only the utterance of a psychical event supposed to be taking place at that very moment, but also, as it were, the reflection of a personal life of such-and-such a kind.

This must, however, be carefully distinguished from another area of seeming whose ontological legitimacy cannot be doubted. I mean the realm of 'genuine seeming', where a lad, for instance, imitates his heroic model and while he is doing so is seized by the actuality of heroism, or a man plays the part of a destiny and conjures up authentic destiny. In this situation there is nothing false; the imitation is genuine imitation and the part played is genuine; the mask, too, is a mask and no deceit. But where the semblance originates from the lie and is permeated by it, the interhuman is threatened in its very existence. It is not that someone utters a lie, falsifies some account. The lie I mean does not take place in relation to particular facts, but in relation to existence itself, and it attacks interhuman existence as such. There are times when a man, to satisfy some stale conceit, forfeits the great chance of a true happening between I and Thou.

Let us now imagine two men, whose life is dominated by appearance, sitting and talking together. Call them Peter and Paul. Let us list the different configurations which are involved. First, there is Peter as he wishes to appear to Paul, and Paul as he wishes to appear to Peter. Then there is Peter as he really appears to Paul, that is, Paul's image of Peter, which in general does not in the least coincide with what Peter wishes Paul to see; and similarly there is the reverse situation. Further, there is Peter as he appears to himself, and Paul as he appears to himself. Lastly, there are the bodily Peter and the bodily Paul. Two living beings and six ghostly appearances, which mingle in many ways in the conversation between the two. Where is there room for any genuine interhuman life?

Whatever the meaning of the word 'truth' may be in other realms, in the interhuman realm it means that men communicate themselves to one another as what they are. It does not depend on one saying to the other everything that occurs to him, but only on his letting no seeming creep in between himself and the other. It does not depend on one letting himself go before another, but on his granting to the man to whom he communicates himself a share in his being. This is a question of the authenticity of the interhuman, and where this is not to be found, neither is the human element itself authentic.

Therefore, as we begin to recognize the crisis of man as the crisis of what is between man and man, we must free the concept of uprightness from the thin moralistic tones which cling to it, and let it take its tone from the concept of bodily uprightness. If a presupposition of human life in primeval times is given in man's walking upright, the fulfilment of human life can only come through the soul's walking upright, through the great uprightness which is not tempted by any seeming because it has conquered all semblance.

But, one may ask, what if a man by his nature makes his life subservient to the images which he produces in others? Can he, in such a case, still become a man living from his being, can he escape from his nature?

The widespread tendency to live from the recurrent impression one makes instead of from the steadiness of one's being is not a 'nature'. It originates, in fact, on the other side of interhuman life itself, in men's dependence upon one another. It is no light thing to be confirmed in one's being by others, and seeming deceptively offers itself as a help in this. To yield to seeming is man's essential cowardice, to resist it is his essential courage. But this is not an inexorable state of affairs which is as it is and must so remain. One can struggle to come to oneself—that is, to come to confidence in being. One struggles, now more successfully, now less, but never in vain, even when one thinks he is defeated. One must at times pay dearly for life lived from the being; but it is never too dear. Yet is there not bad being, do weeds not grow everywhere? I have never known a young person who seemed to me irretrievably bad. Later indeed it becomes more and more difficult to penetrate the increasingly tough layer which has settled down on a man's being. Thus there arises the false perspective of the seemingly fixed 'nature' which cannot be overcome. It is false; the foreground is deceitful; man as man can be redeemed.

Again we see Peter and Paul before us surrounded by the ghosts of the semblances. A ghost can be exorcized. Let us imagine that these two find it more and more repellent to be represented by ghosts. In each of them the will is stirred and strengthened to be confirmed in their being as what they really are and nothing else. We see the forces of real life at work as they drive out the ghosts, till the semblance vanishes and the depths of personal life call to one another.

PERSONAL MAKING PRESENT

By far the greater part of what is today called conversation among men would be more properly and precisely described as speechifying. In general, people do not really speak to one another, but each, although turned to the other, really speaks to a fictitious court of appeal whose life consists of nothing but listening to him. Chekhov has given poetic expression to this state of affairs in *The Cherry Orchard*, where the only use the members of a family make of their being together is to talk past one another. But it is Sartre who has raised to a principle of existence what in Chekhov still appears as the deficiency of a person who is shut up in himself. Sartre regards the walls between the partners in a conversation as simply impassable. For him it is inevitable human destiny that a man has directly to do only with himself and his own affairs. The inner existence of the other is his own concern, not mine; there is no direct relation with the other, nor can there be. This is perhaps the clearest expression of the wretched fatalism of modern man, which regards degeneration as the unchangeable nature of *Homo sapiens* and the misfortune of having run into a blind alley as his primal fate, and which brands every thought of a break-through as reactionary romanticism. He who really knows how far our generation has lost the way of true freedom, of free giving between I and Thou, must himself, by virtue of the demand implicit in every great knowledge of this kind, practise directness—even if he were the only man on earth who did it —and not depart from it until scoffers are struck with fear, and hear in his voice the voice of their own suppressed longing.

The chief presupposition for the rise of genuine dialogue is that each should regard his partner as the very one he is. I become aware of him, aware that he is different, essentially different from myself, in the definite, unique way which is peculiar to him, and I accept whom I thus see, so that in full earnestness I can direct what I say to him as the person he is. Perhaps from time to time I must offer strict opposition to his view about the subject of our conversation. But I accept this person, the personal bearer of a conviction, in his definite being out of which his conviction has grown—even though I must try to show, bit by bit, the wrongness of this very conviction. I affirm the person I struggle with: I struggle with him as his partner, I confirm him as creature and as creation, I confirm him who is opposed to me as him who is over against me. It is true that it now depends on the other whether genuine dia-logue, mutuality in speech arises between us. But if I thus give to the other who confronts me his legitimate standing as a man with whom I am ready to enter into dialogue, then I may trust him and suppose him to be also ready to deal with me as his partner.

But what does it mean to be 'aware' of a man in the exact sense in which I use the word? To be aware of a thing or a being means, in quite general terms, to experience it as a whole and yet at the same time without reduction or abstraction, in all its concreteness. But a man, although he exists as a living being among living beings and even as a thing among things, is nevertheless something categorically different from all things and all beings. A man cannot really be grasped except on the basis of the gift of the spirit which belongs to man alone among all things, the spirit as sharing decisively in the personal life of the living man, that is, the spirit which determines the person. To be aware of a man, therefore, means in particular to perceive his wholeness as a person determined by the spirit; it means to perceive the dynamic centre which stamps his every utterance, action, and attitude with the recognizable sign of uniqueness. Such an awareness is impossible, however, if and so long as the other is the separated object of my contemplation or even observation, for this wholeness and its centre do not let themselves be known to contemplation or observation. It is only possible when I step into an elemental relation with the other, that is, when he becomes present to me. Hence I designate awareness in this special sense as 'personal making present'.

The perception of one's fellow man as a whole, as a unity, and as unique—even if his wholeness, unity, and uniqueness are only partly developed, as is usually the case—is opposed in our time by almost everything that is commonly understood as specifically modern. In our time there predominates an analytical, reductive, and deriving look between man and man. This look is analytical, or rather pseudo analytical, since it treats the whole being as put together and therefore able to be taken apart—not only the so-called unconscious which is accessible to relative objectification, but also the psychic stream itself, which can never, in fact, be grasped as an object. This look is a reductive one because it tries to contract the manifold person, who is nourished by the microcosmic richness of the possible, to some schematically surveyable and recurrent structures. And this look is a deriving one because it supposes it can grasp what a man has become, or even is becoming, in genetic formulae, and it thinks that even the dynamic central principle of the individual in this becoming can be represented by a general concept. An effort is being made today radically to destroy the mystery between man and man. The personal life, the ever near mystery, once the source of the stillest enthusiasms, is levelled down.

What I have just said is not an attack on the analytical method of the human sciences, a method which is indispensable wherever it furthers knowledge of a phenomenon without impairing the essentially different knowledge of its uniqueness that transcends the valid circle of the method. The science of man that makes use of the analytical method must accordingly always keep in view the boundary of such a contemplation, which stretches like a horizon around it. This duty makes the transposition of the method into life dubious; for it is excessively difficult to see where the boundary is in life.

If we want to do today's work and prepare tomorrow's with clear sight, then we must develop in ourselves and in the next generation a gift which lives in man's inwardness as a Cinderella, one day to be a princess. Some call it intuition, but that is not a wholly unambiguous concept. I prefer the name 'imagining the real', for in its essential being this gift is not a looking at the other, but a bold swinging—demanding the most intensive stirring of one's being—into the life of the other. This is the nature of all genuine imagining, only that here the realm of my action is not the all-possible, but the particular real person who confronts me, whom I can attempt to make present to myself just in this way, and not otherwise, in his wholeness, unity, and uniqueness, and with his dynamic centre which realizes all these things ever anew.

Let it be said again that all this can only take place in a living partnership, that is, when I stand in a common situation with the other and expose myself vitally to his share in the situation as really his share. It is true that my basic attitude can remain unanswered, and the dialogue can die in seed. But if mutuality stirs, then the interhuman blossoms into genuine dialogue.

71

IMPOSITION AND UNFOLDING

I have referred to two things which impede the growth of life between men: the invasion of seeming, and the inadequacy of perception. We are now faced with a third, plainer than the others, and in this critical hour more powerful and more dangerous than ever.

There are two basic ways of affecting men in their views and their attitude to life. In the first a man tries to impose himself, his opinion and his attitude, on the other in such a way that the latter feels the psychical result of the action to be his own insight, which has only been freed by the influence. In the second basic way of affecting others, a man wishes to find and to further in the soul of the other the disposition toward what he has recognized in himself as the right. Because it is the right, it must also be alive in the microcosm of the other, as one possibility. The other need only be opened out in this potentiality of his; moreover, this opening out takes place not essentially by teaching, but by meeting, by existential communication between someone that is in actual being and someone that is in a process of becoming. The first way has been most powerfully developed in the realm of propaganda, the second in that of education.

The propagandist I have in mind, who imposes himself, is not in the least concerned with the person whom he desires to influence, as a person; various individual qualities are of importance only in so far as he can exploit them to win the other and must get to know them for this purpose. In his indifference to everything personal the propagandist goes a substantial distance beyond the party for which he works. For the party, persons in their difference are of significance because each can be used according to his special qualities in a particular function. It is true that the personal is considered only in respect of the specific use to which it can be put, but within these limits it is recognized in practice. To propaganda as such, on the other hand, individual qualities are rather looked on as a burden, for propaganda is concerned simply with *more*—more members, more adherents, an increasing extent of support. Political methods, where they rule in an extreme form, as here, simply

72

mean winning power over the other by depersonalizing him. This kind of propaganda enters upon different relations with force; it supplements it or replaces it, according to the need or the prospects, but it is in the last analysis nothing but sublimated violence, which has become imperceptible as such. It places men's souls under a pressure which allows the illusion of autonomy. Political methods at their height mean the effective abolition of the human factor.

The educator whom I have in mind lives in a world of individuals, a certain number of whom are always at any one time committed to his care. He sees each of these individuals as in a position to become a unique, single person, and thus the bearer of a special task of existence which can be fulfilled through him and through him alone. He sees every personal life as engaged in such a process of actualization, and he knows from his own experience that the forces making for actualization are all the time involved in a microcosmic struggle with counterforces. He has come to see himself as a helper of the actualizing forces. He knows these forces; they have shaped and they still shape him. Now he puts this person shaped by them at their disposal for a new struggle and a new work. He cannot wish to impose himself, for he believes in the effect of the actualizing forces, that is, he believes that in every man what is right is established in a single and uniquely personal way. No other way may be imposed on a man, but another way, that of the educator, may and must unfold what is right, as in this case it struggles for achievement, and help it to develop.

The propagandist, who imposes himself, does not really believe even in his own cause, for he does not trust it to attain its effect of its own power without his special methods, whose symbols are the loudspeaker and the television advertisement. The educator who unfolds what is there believes in the primal power which has scattered itself, and still scatters itself, in all human beings in order that it may grow up in each man in the special form of that man. He is confident that this growth needs at each moment only that help which is given in meeting, and that he is called to supply that help.

I have illustrated the character of the two basic attitudes and their relation to one another by means of two extremely antithetical examples. But wherever men have dealings with one another, one or the other attitude is to be found in more or less degree.

These two principles of imposing oneself on someone and helping someone to unfold should not be confused with concepts such as arrogance and humility. A man can be arrogant without wishing to impose himself on others, and it is not enough to be humble in order to help another unfold. Arrogance and humility are dispositions of the soul, psychological facts with a moral accent, while imposition and helping to unfold are events between men, anthropological facts which point to an ontology, the ontology of the interhuman.

In the moral realm Kant expressed the essential principle that one's fellow man must never be thought of and treated merely as a means, but always at the same time as an independent end. The principle is expressed as an 'ought' which is sustained by the idea of human dignity. My point of view, which is near to Kant's in its essential features, has another source and goal. It is concerned with the presuppositions of the interhuman. Man exists anthropologically not in his isolation, but in the completeness of the relation between man and man; what humanity is can be properly grasped only in vital reciprocity. For the proper existence of the interhuman it is necessary, as I have shown, that the semblance not intervene to spoil the relation of personal being to personal being. It is further necessary, as I have also shown, that each one means and makes present the other in his personal being. That neither should wish to impose himself on the other is the third basic presupposition of the interhuman. These presuppositions do not include the demand that one should influence the other in his unfolding; this is, however, an element that is suited to lead to a higher stage of the interhuman.

That there resides in every man the possibility of attaining authentic human existence in the special way peculiar to him can be grasped in the Aristotelian image of entelechy, innate self-realization; but one must note that it is an entelechy of the work of creation. It would be mistaken to speak here of individuation alone. Individuation is only the indispensable personal stamp of all realization of human existence. The self as such is not ultimately the essential, but the meaning of human existence given in creation again and again fulfils itself as self. The help that men give each other in becoming a self leads the life between men to its height. The dynamic glory of the being of man is first bodily present in the relation between two men each of whom in meaning the other also means the highest to which this person is called, and serves the self-realization of this human life as one true to creation without wishing to impose on the other anything of his own realization.

GENUINE DIALOGUE

We must now summarize and clarify the marks of genuine dialogue.

In genuine dialogue the turning to the partner takes place in all truth, that is, it is a turning of the being. Every speaker 'means' the partner or partners to whom he turns as this personal existence. To 'mean' someone in this connection is at the same time to exercise that degree of making present which is possible to the speaker at that moment. The experiencing senses and the imagining of the real which completes the findings of the senses work together to make the other present as a whole and as a unique being, as the person that he is. But the speaker does not merely perceive the one who is present to him in this way; he receives him as his partner, and that means that he confirms this other being, so far as it is for him to confirm. The true turning of his person to the other includes this confirmation, this acceptance. Of course, such a confirmation does not mean approval; but no matter in what I am against the other, by accepting him as my partner in genuine dialogue I have affirmed him as a person.

Further, if genuine dialogue is to arise, everyone who takes part in it must bring himself into it. And that also means that he must be willing on each occasion to say what is really in his mind about the subject of the conversation. And that means further that on each occasion he makes the contribution of his spirit without reduction and without shifting his ground. Even men of great integrity are under the illusion that they are not bound to say everything 'they have to say'. But in the great faithfulness which is the climate of genuine dialogue, what I have to say at any one time already has in me the character of something that wishes to be uttered, and I must not keep it back, keep it in myself. It bears for me the unmistakable sign which indicates that it belongs to the common life of the word. Where the dialogical word genuinely exists, it must be given its right by keeping nothing back. To keep nothing back is the exact opposite of unreserved speech. Everything depends on the legitimacy of 'what I have to say'. And of course I must also be intent to raise into an inner word and then into a spoken word what I have to say at this moment but do not yet possess as speech. To speak is both nature and work, something that grows and something that is made, and where it appears dialogically, in the climate of great faithfulness, it has to fulfill ever anew the unity of the two.

Associated with this is that overcoming of semblance to which I have referred. In the atmosphere of genuine dialogue, he who is ruled by the thought of his own effect as the speaker of what he has to speak, has a destructive effect. If instead of what has to be said, I try to bring attention to my *I*, I have irrevocably miscarried what I had to say; it enters the dialogue as a failure, and the dialogue is a failure. Because genuine dialogue is an ontological sphere which is constituted by the authenticity of being, every invasion of semblance must damage it.

But where the dialogue is fulfilled in its being, between partners who have turned to one another in truth, who express themselves without reserve and are free of the desire for semblance, there is brought into being a memorable common fruitfulness which is to be found nowhere else. At such times, at each such time, the word arises in a substantial way between men who have been seized in their depths and opened out by the dynamic of an elemental togetherness. The interhuman opens out what otherwise remains unopened.

This phenomenon is indeed well known in dialogue between two persons; but I have also sometimes experienced it in a dialogue in which several have taken part.

About Easter of 1914 there met a group consisting of representatives of several European nations for a three-day

discussion that was intended to be preliminary to further talks.[1]
We wanted to discuss together how the catastrophe, which we
all believed was imminent, could be avoided. Without our
having agreed beforehand on any sort of modalities for our
talk, all the presuppositions of genuine dialogue were fulfilled.
From the first hour immediacy reigned between all of us, some
of whom had just got to know one another; everyone spoke
with an unheard-of unreserve, and clearly not a single one of
the participants was in bondage to semblance. In respect of its
purpose the meeting must be described as a failure (though
even now in my heart it is still not a certainty that it had to be
a failure); the irony of the situation was that we arranged the
final discussion for the middle of August, and in the course of
events the group was soon broken up. Nevertheless, in the
time that followed, not one of the participants doubted that he
shared in a triumph of the interhuman.

One more point must be noted. Of course it is not necessary
for all who are joined in a genuine dialogue actually to speak;
those who keep silent can on occasion be especially important.
But each must be determined not to withdraw when the course
of the conversation makes it proper for him to say what he
has to say. No one, of course, can know in advance what it is
that he has to say; genuine dialogue cannot be arranged beforehand. It has indeed its basic order in itself from the beginning,
but nothing can be determined, the course is of the spirit, and
some discover what they have to say only when they catch
the call of the spirit.

But it is also a matter of course that all the participants,
without exception, must be of such nature that they are capable
of satisfying the presuppositions of genuine dialogue and are
ready to do so. The genuineness of the dialogue is called in
question as soon as even a small number of those present are
felt by themselves and by the others as not being expected to
take any active part. Such a state of affairs can lead to very
serious problems.

I had a friend whom I account one of the most considerable
men of our age. He was a master of conversation, and he loved

---

[1] I have set down elsewhere an episode from this meeting. See my essay
'Dialogue' in *Between Man and Man*, especially pp. 4–6.

it: his genuineness as a speaker was evident. But once it happened that he was sitting with two friends and with the three wives, and a conversation arose in which by its nature the women were clearly not joining, although their presence in fact had a great influence. The conversation among the men soon developed into a duel between two of them (I was the third). The other 'duelist', also a friend of mine, was of a noble nature; he too was a man of true conversation, but given more to objective fairness than to the play of the intellect, and a stranger to any controversy. The friend whom I have called a master of conversation did not speak with his usual composure and strength, but he scintillated, he fought, he triumphed. The dialogue was destroyed.

CHAPTER IV

WHAT IS COMMON TO ALL[1]

Among the sayings with which Heracleitus laid the foundation of the edifice of Western thought, there is one of such great simplicity, one which appears to us latecomers of the spirit so self-evident that we are accustomed to understand it as only meant metaphorically. What is more, Heracleitus himself in other sayings appears to relate to it in such a manner. But at this height nothing concrete persists that is only metaphor, nothing that does not also have a complete existence as the expression of the direct contemplation of a perceived reality.

The saying reads, 'The waking have a single cosmos in common', that is, a single world-shape in which they take part in common. By this is already expressed what the later moral philosopher Plutarch, who preserved the fragment for us, pointed to in his interpretation: In sleep each turns away from the common cosmos and turns to something which belongs to him alone, something thus which he does not and cannot share with any other. That Heracleitus himself, on the contrary, understood this less as the sleep of an individual, including the sphere of dreams, than as a cosmos, one among numberless fleeting world-shapes, in no way corresponds to what we know of his teachings.

The duality of sleeping and waking is not, as elsewhere in Heracleitus, a symbol of the duality of that man who is aware of his being and its meaning and all the others who live alienated from it. There is here what is always necessary in order

[1] Trans. by Maurice Friedman.

that a genuine symbol can take shape in the spirit—an existent corporeal reality which is grasped in a decisive vision. The philosopher of Ephesus makes manifest for the Occident the fundamental insight that the rhythmically regulated course of our daily existence does not mean an exchange of two states, but an exchange of two spheres in which we find ourselves by turns, and one of which Heracleitus calls a cosmos.

Heracleitus designates this one cosmos, which he as an evaluating thinker affirms, as one common to men. But it means something other and greater than that they all dwell together in the sphere that we call the world or that each of them is given just this sphere to perceive. 'The common' is the sustaining category for Heracleitus. It enables him, despite men's want of understanding—so painfully suffered and so fiercely reproved by him—to grasp and confirm as a spiritual reality their together-ness, the full mutuality of human being. When Heracleitus says of the logos, the meaning of being that dwells in the substance of the word, that it is common, he thereby asserts that all men in the eternal originality of their genuine spoken intercourse with one another have a share in the consummation of this indwelling. This is the case with the world-shape which belongs to the whole of the human race, the 'common cosmos'. The same meaning of existence which holds sway in the coming-to-be of the words, the same genuineness for ever renewing itself in the fire of oppositeness is that which embodies itself in the world process. But this world, which Heracleitus understands as the world of man, never arises except out of the totality of the human race to which it belongs. Men contribute to the cosmic process with all that they are. Even in sleep, according to Heracleitus—no matter though each is submerged in his private sphere—they are still, as individuals, 'workers and co-workers in the world-happening', passive workers. This means that there is no state in which the individual merely leads his own existence without contributing his part, just through living in this state, to the life of his human environment and to the world in general. But waking men add in common to the world-shape itself, which is just a human cosmos recognizable as the cosmos of man as man. They associate with one another in the world, helping one another through the power of the logos to grasp the world as a world order, without which ordering grasp it is not and cannot be a world. They can only do this, of course, if and in so far as they are truly awake, if they do not sleep while waking and spin dreamlike illusions which they call their own insight—if they exist in common.

'One must follow that which is common.' This great saying of Heracleitus discloses its meaning to us only when we have considered his teaching of the community of the logos and the cosmos. Waking and sleeping are one of the pairs of opposites in which the unity of being fulfils itself, according to Heracleitus, swinging in them and bearing their tension. In each pair each of the two opposites has its own place and its own right. But the effacement of the tension and the mixture of the opposites is evil. This is also the case with waking and sleeping. In sleep there is no factual bond with others; each dreams of the others, but those of whom he dreams do not take part in his dream. Conversely, that dream condition in which each is to himself alone must not penetrate into the common world of waking. Here and only here are we 'We'. Here as men awake we may understand the logos by understanding one another in our truth, through whose voice the logos speaks. Here we are actively familiar with the cosmos through our co-operation, for it is a cosmos only to the degree in which we experience it together. Heracleitus places upon us the pure duty and responsibility of waking togetherness. He does not, of course, reject the dream, which has its place and its right in that withdrawnness inaccessible to the We. But he does reject that dreamlike refusal of the We through whose illusion the common day is broken asunder.

2

With his proclamation of the world-shape assigned to the waking and of the meaning of being which is represented in it as the common that we must follow, Heracleitus has indicated to the spirit the task of showing itself awake in the human world, and that means the task of establishing in common a common reality. What that signifies in the history of the spirit can be made clear by two examples of the opposite.

In the same age in which the Asia Minor Greek, Heracleitus, established the right and duty of the waking spirit, China received, mostly through oral tradition, the decisive imprint of a teaching which was at once notably similar and notably dissimilar to his. This is the teaching of Tao, the Way, which is itself unconditional unity, yet bears, encompasses, and rhythmically regulates the alternation of the opposites and opposing processes, their correspondences and contradictions, their battles and their couplings. This happens in the world as in the spirit, for just as with Heracleitus, so here, they both belong to one order. But the opposites themselves do not stand here in the irreducible multiplicity of fire and water, day and night, life and death as they do for Heracleitus. Rather all these and their like are only appearances and acts of the two primal essences, yin and yang. These essences manifest themselves as the feminine and the masculine, the dark and the light, the loose and the fast, the yielding and the advancing, in short, as nonbeing and being. They supplement each other, wed each other; indeed, in the Tao Te King (which appears, despite the uncertainty of the traditions, to have preserved much of the oldest level of speech of the teaching) it is even said that being and nonbeing generate each other. Here, however, in contrast to Heracleitus, the passive principle is accorded the preeminence because it is the truly effective one. What this implies about the sphere of waking and that of dreams is shown with the utmost clarity in a text of Chuang Tzu, a thinker and poet of the fourth century who considered himself a late-born disciple of Lao Tze, the master by then wholly inwoven in legend.

Chuang Tzu reports a dream and its sequel. He speaks of himself in the third person.

Chuang Chou dreamed once that he was a butterfly, a butterfly fluttering hither and thither without care and desire, unconscious of his existence as Chuang Chou. Suddenly he awoke, and he lay there, again the self-same Chuang Chou. Now he does not know: is he a man who dreamed that he was a butterfly or a butterfly who dreams that he is a man?[1]

[1] Martin Buber, *Reden und Gleichnisse des Tschuang-Tse* (Leipzig: Insel-Verlag, 1914).

This text is not isolated. Another Taoist book tells of a mythical realm at whose borders the play of the opposites grows lame. There is no difference between cold and hot, between night and day. The inhabitants, who need neither food nor clothing, sleep for seven weeks. When they then awaken, they hold what they have dreamed to be real and what they now experience to be only apparent.

In this reaching, obviously, no priority belongs to the waking existence; indeed, if one of the two spheres were to be claimed as world, it might much more easily be that of dreams, and this just for the reason that the awakened are able to recognize it as dream whereas the waker's circle of experience pretends to be simple reality without being able to support this claim.

Logos and cosmos are not valid here. But the common also is not valid here. The human person in his withdrawal obtains the full measure of his allotted existence.

In the same section in which the mythical realm is told of, we read how a frail servant was cruelly treated by his master, but dreamed night after night that he was a prince and lived in joy, and therefore was also content with his lot by day, whereas the opposite befell the master. And yet another story from the same section pictures Lao Tze as treating even madness with similar composure. 'If the whole world were insane except for you,' he says to the complaining father of a mentally ill son, 'then it would be just you who would be the insane one.'

Thus it stands here concerning the antithetical spheres in the life of man. What we wakers hold to be a dreamlike delusion is here valid as just as real as the waking world, indeed as more real. The other sphere stands ready to receive man, and even comfortingly and graciously. But just not us, rather only each individual among us separately. We, as We, cannot enter it; it receives no We. Each of us dreams that he associates with others; but none of these others experiences this in itself, none enters the dream sphere with us. The claim of the special realm to be a world is that against which Heracleitus poses his elemental saying: 'One must follow that which is common.'

3

The other manifestation out of the depths of the East is more far-reaching. It is a teaching of the oldest Upanishads, which means a teaching originally strictly esoteric, proceeding at times from the mouth of the master to the ears of the disciples who sit at his feet, the teaching of dream sleep and deep sleep.

The dream is generally regarded here as a first step. The spirit of the person is depicted as he, after entering into the dream sleep, roams all over the whole world and gathers his building materials which he 'splits up', that is, divides into their elementary parts in order to build out of them 'in his own light' what he can build, for 'he is a creator'. Verses, clearly of still older origin than the prose teaching, are quoted in which it is said:

> That lower nest, the breath must guard it,
> He springs away immortal from the nest,
> Immortal roves about, where he wills,
> The golden spirit, the solitary wandering goose.
> In the state of dreams he roves up and down
> And fashions for himself, godlike, all kinds of shapes.

The sovereign freedom of the dream is praised more strongly here than in the Taoist texts. All ties of the day are suspended. Self-glorious moulder, the spirit fashions the whole world, subject to him as unresisting material. He needs for his work no other light than his own, and in divine power of transformation he clothes himself in shape after shape.

But now the sovereign spirit ascends beyond the sphere of dreams. He finds no more satisfaction in the play of transformations; he gives up the last tie with the world, that of the images taken from it, and enters into the fully dreamless, imageless, desireless deep sleep. 'As in the air', continues that text, 'a falcon or an eagle, weary of flight, folding its pinions, prepares to spiral down, thus the essential spirit hurries to that sleeping state where it wishes no wish and beholds no dream.' Drawn forth from all shapes by which it was related to the material of the world, it has now attained a shapeless abiding in worldless being. Only then, enclosed and hidden in this state, is it, as is said further on, 'beyond desire, untroubled by ills, free of anxiety', to all of which it was still exposed, in fact, in the dream world despite its absence of ties. He no longer experiences now what was separate from, separable from himself, for 'there is no second outside of him'. Another text, which stems out of the same oldest epoch of Upanishads, describes the same thing. 'When it is said', we read here, 'that a man sleeps'—by which it is just deep sleep that is meant—'he is united with being. He has entered into his self. Where one sees no other, hears no other, recognizes no other, this is the fullness.'

We must pay close attention to what is said in this statement which in the West has had far-reaching effects in our age.

Sleep appears here as the way out of the sphere in which man is divided from the kernel of being to that in which he is united with it. The way leads beyond the freedom which unfolds in dreams to unity. This unity is that of the individual self with the Self of being: they are in reality a single self. Their dis-union in the waking world is then the great illusion. We become independent of the waking world in dream and yet remain still imprisoned in it; in deep sleep we become free of it and thereby of illusion, which alone divides the personal self from the Self of being—an inference, to be sure, which was first conclusively drawn in later, more specifically philosophical teachings. According to them, the existence of man in the world is the existence of a world of appearance, a magical deception. But since the identity of the self can be reached only in an absolute solitude, such as deep sleep, the existence between man and man is also ultimately only appearance and illusion.

The saying 'That art thou', which later ages have extended to the relation between man and man, is solely intended in the original teaching for the relation between Brahman and Atman, the Self of being and the self of the human person. Even though each man experiences the identity of all selves in deep sleep, he cannot establish it in the waking world, in the world of appearance. In one of the Upanishadic texts cited here, being embraced by a beloved wife serves as a parable of unification; but considered as a fact of life, it is relegated to illusion. The man who adheres to the teaching of identity may, of course, when he says 'Thou' to a fellow man, say to himself in reference to the other, 'There are you yourself', for he believes the self of the other to be identical with his. But what the genuine saying of 'Thou' to the other in the reality of the common existence basically means—namely, the affirmation of the primally deep otherness of the other, the affirmation of his otherness which is accepted and loved by me—this is devalued and destroyed in spirit through just that identification. The teaching of identity not only stands in opposition to the belief in the true being of a common logos and a common cosmos; it also contradicts the arch reality of that out of which all community stems—human meeting.

When taken seriously in the factual, waking continuity of intercourse with one another, the ancient Hindu 'That art thou' becomes the postulate of an annihilation of the human person, one's own person as well as the other; for the person is through and through nothing other than uniqueness and thus essentially other than all that is over against it. And even if that supposed universal Self should remain in the ground of the I, it could no longer have intercourse with anyone. But we see in human existence, in the intercourse of men with one another that grows out of it, the chance for meeting between existing being and existing being. In this meeting each of the two certainly does not say to himself, 'He over there is you', but perhaps each says to the other, 'I accept you as you are'. Here first is uncurtailed existence.

4

The object of this juxtaposition of the sayings of Heracleitus with the sayings of the Taoist masters and of the early Upanishads is no historical one, but neither is it concerned with a critical comparison of the Orient and the Occident. The stretch of earth between the Black and the Red seas in which, in the same epoch, Anaximander and Heracleitus taught in Greek and the Israelite prophets admonished and comforted in Hebrew, must not be understood as a wall but as a bridge between East and West. The teachings of those philosophers —the teaching that all beings owe one another atonement, and the teaching of the community of logos and cosmos—and the message of those who proclaimed that all men owe help to one another and announced the task of communal life, both arose from the heart of the East and both have contributed essentially to the foundation of the spirit of the West.

If I appeal to the philosophy of Heracleitus, shot through with contradictions as it appears, against the uniformly soaring wisdom of the Orient, it is for the sake of a specific need of our time. I mean by this the confrontation of two points of view, the first of which values the collectivity above all else, whereas the second believes the meaning of existence to be disclosed or disclosable in the relation of the individual to his self. The first, which is usually called the Eastern because it is today especially at home in Eastern Europe, appears to be a travesty of the ancient idea of the common way; the second, represented by Western philosophy, psychology, and literature, readily invokes the ancient Indian teaching and its offshoots. This latter I am discussing, and the reasons for this choice are weighty ones. The modern collectivism does, in fact, place the collectivity above all, but it does not ascribe to it the character of the absolute; it treats the absolute in general as an inadmissible fiction. The modern variety of individualism, in contrast, is inclined to understand the individual self, which the I finds in its depth, as the self simply and as the absolute. Despite all stress on the interest in the 'outer world' or even a kind of cosmic sympathy, despite all reference to the all-soul as the one that is really meant, what unmistakably rules here is the tendency toward the primacy of the individual existence and toward its self-glorification. And this individualism is still more dangerous than collectivism, for the pretension of the false absolute is more dangerous than the denial of the absolute.

Let us call to mind once more the vital originality of the three basic concepts of Heracleitus: the concept of the common, of the logos, and of the cosmos; and, starting from their originality, let us endeavour to penetrate into our situation. Heracleitus says of thinking that it is common to all, and he elucidates this by the statement that all men take part in thinking as well as in self-knowledge. The concreteness of his observation, which he preserves even in the highest abstractions, indicates that this does not mean the universally known fact that each of us possesses the capacity of thinking, but that when we know and think in accordance with the logos, we do so not in isolation but in common: we blend all our particular knowing and even in our knowledge of ourselves one person helps the other. This communality in which we participate, living with one another and acting on one another, this 'one must follow'.

Heracleitus always remained in accord with the thoroughly sensuous living speech of his time. For this reason the logos, even in its highest sublimation, does not cease to be for him the sensuous, meaningful word, the human talk which contains the meaning of the true. Meaning can be in the word because it is in being. Thus it stirs deep in the soul which becomes aware of the meaning; it grows in it and develops out of it to a voice which speaks to fellow souls and is heard by them, often, to be sure, without this hearing becoming a real receiving. And like the logos, so also the cosmos belongs to the common as to that in which men participate as in a common work. That it is common to them does not signify the likewise universally known fact that they find themselves together in the world; it signifies that their relationship to it is a common one. What is spoken of as the subjective side of our perceptions, however, is certainly not rendered uncertain by this insight of Heracleitus. For we can indeed show one another the things, describe for one another the things; each can, supplementing the other, help him to have a world-shape, a world.

There is more to be said about this. But first let us examine a variety of this individualism which is of interest as an example. The tendency to attain a higher side of existence, indeed the 'authentic' existence, through abandoning the communal finds here an especially drastic expression. The advocates of the undertaking intend, it is true, to be removed therein from what they call 'the world of selfhood', but in reality they are intent throughout upon isolating the sphere reserved for the individual and with it that of selfhood. The occurrences of this province are much more easily communicable than what takes place in the purely inward way, especially at its end, and thus there is some material available to us.

5

Not long ago the English novelist Aldous Huxley described and extolled the astonishing effects of mescalin intoxication. Mescalin is extracted from a cactus, the enjoyment of which so ravished and enraptured some ancient Mexican Indian tribes that they made the bounteous plant the centre of an elaborate cult. Huxley reports the effects of the intoxication from his own experience, which took place under the watch of disciplined self-observation.

What he saw there with open eyes was not some sort of world-removed fantasy structure. It was his familiar domestic surroundings, loosened from their spatial limitations in un-dreamed-of brilliance of colour and an overpowering presence of the individual object, which Huxley compares with the cubist way of seeing. But this radical aestheticizing of the relationship to things is only the first step toward a higher kind of vision which he describes as 'the sacramental vision of reality'. To the religions, sacrament means the participation, verified in life and death, of the whole person who has known the contact of the transcendent in his corporeal existence. But Huxley means by sacramental vision merely penetrating and being received into the depths of the world of the senses. In his view, the shadow realm, held together by concepts that we call reality, falls to pieces there, for it is unmasked as 'the universe of a diminished consciousness', and this diminished conscious-ness is just that which comes to expression in speech. 'Through the taking of a suitable chemical preparation', so Huxley says, everyone is enabled 'to know from within of what the mystics speak'; the speechless primal ground of being opens itself to him in the objects. No distinction exists any longer between inner and outer, between subject and object. Naturally Huxley must avoid the eyes of those present in the room, people who are otherwise especially dear to him; they belong, indeed, to the 'world of selfhood' that he has left.

With this concept he describes, without naming it, the common world. When he speaks of the mescalin trance as one of the different kinds of 'flight out of selfhood and environment', to which flight the urge is 'present in almost every man at almost every time', then he means again the common world from which the enjoyer of mescalin flees for the duration of his trance. Huxley calls it, to be sure, the 'urge to go beyond the self', by which he means that here man escapes the entanglement in the net of his utilitarian aims. But in reality the consumer of mescalin does not emerge from this net into some sort of free participation in common being; rather merely into a strictly private special sphere given to him as his own for several hours. The 'chemical holidays' of which Huxley speaks are holidays not only from the petty I, enmeshed in the machinery of its aims, but also from the person participating in the community of logos and cosmos—holidays from the very uncomfortable reminder to verify oneself as such a person.

Huxley speaks also of holidays from the possibly repugnant surroundings. But man may master as he will his situation, to which his surroundings also belong; he may withstand it, he may alter it, he may, when it is necessary, exchange it for another; but the fugitive flight out of the claim of the situation into situationlessness is no legitimate affair of man. And the true name of all the paradises which man creates for himself by chemical or other means is situationlessness. They are situationless like the dream state and like schizophrenia because they are in their essence uncommunal, while every situation, even the situation of those who enter into solitude, is enclosed in the community of logos and cosmos.

The men with whom we live also belong to that environment from which, in Huxley's view, it is desirable and salutary to take holidays of the soul from time to time. If we have taken a sufficient dose of mescalin, then the objects of our environment are transformed into sheer glory; but the men who directly surround us are not transformed with them. It is logical therefore, as Huxley relates, that he now avoids their eyes; to regard each other means to recognize the common. It may be that the Indians who enjoyed the peyotl cactus looked at one another as much as before; the modern civilized man in this state turns his eyes away from the men of his surroundings since they belong to the world which formerly bound him.

We read something similar in many reports of experimental subjects about their mescalin trances. They relate how, 'near to the "thing in itself" ' they found themselves floating above all, removed from the 'painful earthly world', and also experienced as 'kingly play' what they afterward determined to be 'hallucinations'. And it is only the other side of the same coin that they met their fellow men who were present with a deep mistrust, that the organs of strongest contact in their own body, such as the inner surface of the hand and the genital region, felt frozen; that hearing, the sense of mental communication, often seemed to be almost blocked out, that at times, indeed, they could not even succeed in picturing to themselves men in general. This 'feeling of being completely isolated' was once caught in the words, 'There did not need to be any women and also no men'. Many of these traits recall similar basic attitudes of schizophrenics, except that in the case of the latter we discover now and then the longing to alienate from the vile common world individual men who are of particular importance to them and to carry them off into the special world which is alone reliable and meaningful to them.

6

Huxley distinguishes, as mentioned, two stages within the trance.

In the first, one sees the things from within, as the creating artist sees them, at once objectively deepened and transfigured by an inner light. In the second, from which he looks down almost scornfully on his beloved art as on an *ersatz*, one experiences to some degree what the mystics experience.

In fact, the artist too is removed from the common seeing in his decisive moments and raised into his special formative seeing; but in just these moments he is determined through and through, to his perception itself, by the drive to originate, by the command to form. Huxley understands this manner of seeing everything in brilliant coloration and penetrating objectivity not only as 'how one should see', but also as 'how things are in reality'. What does that mean concretely? What we call reality always appears only in our personal contact with things which remain unperceived by us in their own being; and there exists personal contact which, freer, more direct than the ordinary, represents things with greater force, freshness, and depth. This is true of creative states and it is also true of toxic states, but the fundamental distinction between the former and the latter is that the enjoyer of mescalin, for instance, produces the alteration of his consciousness arbitrarily; the vocation of the artist, in contrast, sets him in his unarbitrary special relation to existing being, and from there, willing what he should, he does his work in conscious realization. Where arbitrariness interferes, the art becomes illegitimate.

The same problem comes to light in the second of the stages described—or rather indicated—by Huxley. He says that the mescalin trance enables one 'to know from within of what the visionary, the medium, yes even the mystic speaks'. Let us leave to one side the problematic medium and content ourselves with the observation of the great visions and mystical experiences of human history so far as they are accessible to our observation. One thing is common to all of them: He to whom this happens is overtaken by something from a sphere in which he does not dwell and could not dwell, a 'face', a 'hand', a 'word', a 'mystery'. He is not in accord with it; indeed, he often enough resists what accosts him. He clings to the common world until he is torn from it. And that is by no means a secondary trait, it is the essence of the occurrence itself. The shaman, the yogi have their methods through whose practice they acquire, or imagine they acquire, power of magic and power of absorption; the man of whom we speak has nothing other than his way on which he is assaulted, on which he is led. What takes place here is no flight: one is seized, one is overpowered, one is called.

Neither the artist nor the mystic transposes himself into the condition in which, from time to time, he beholds the vision; he receives it. They do not take themselves out of the communality, they are taken out. And they must deliver up not less than themselves, the whole living person and his whole personal life, in order to withstand what has taken possession of them.

7

The great teachings from which we have proceeded, that of the Asia Minor bridge and that of the Far East, resemble each other in that in both of them the spirit places its claim on the whole of the personal existence, and this claim is only seemingly separable from the teaching. They demand without remainder the life of him who hears it. The early Upanishads point to the objective unification of the self of the soul and the Self of being which arises out of the cessation of consciousness in deep sleep. This unity, the claim is made, shall be fulfilled afterward by the waking, fully conscious, knowing person out of conscious existence, through identifying his own self with that of the world.

The teaching of Lao-tze points to the Tao of heaven, which governs the swinging cosmic opposites, as to the primal image that man shall imitate and can imitate if he is aware of the Tao that dwells in himself, the Tao of man. He shall and can reconcile and wed with each other the conflicting opposites of existence without neutralizing them. For this teaching, too, no less than the whole personal existence will do: the existence which does not interfere but radiates. Both teachings wish to lead men out of the entanglement in the common to the freedom of detachment, that of the Upanishads into the solitude above the world, that of Taoism into the solitude in the midst of the world.

In contrast to both of them stands Heracleitus' teaching that bids one follow that which is common; but the existential claim of the spirit on the person is here actually of still greater weight. Just because, unlike those Indians, Heracleitus' teaching accepts the being of what is in all its manifoldness and knows no other harmony than that which arises out of its tensions, and just because, unlike those Chinese, he finds the meaning of being not in the ground of separateness but in what is common to all, the existential claim is here so direct. Heracleitus' angry reprimand is aimed at the man who hears his word but does not yet truly understand it. It is not he himself that men must understand, he says, but the logos that is common to them all and that makes use of the man Heracleitus in order to enter between them into the spokenness. The logos is certainly not alien to them: indeed, as Heracleitus says, they continually have the closest intercourse with it, with the word, in that they always, in fact, take it in their mouth; and yet they live in discord with it because they always misuse the meaningful word and pervert its sense into nonsense.

For, it must be emphasized yet again, the Heracleitian concept of logos cannot be understood otherwise than from the primal establishment of the wedding between meaning and speech. It is hammered at us three and four times in the fragments that have been preserved: logos is something that is to be heard but is misheard and that should be heard in the right way, as word-with-meaning. It seems incorrect to me to translate logos in oversimplified fashion as 'meaning' whereby its original concreteness is given up; nor can I agree when, from an especially competent quarter, it is interpreted, 'Not with me, rather with the logos in yourselves, must you agree', whereas Heracleitus simply says, 'Do not listen to me but to the logos'. Each soul does, of course, have its logos deep in itself, but the logos does not attain to its fullness in us but rather between us; for it means the eternal chance for speech to become true between men. Therefore, it is common to them.

To man as man belongs the ever renewed event of the entrance of meaning into the living word. Heracleitus demands of the human person that he preserve this occurrence in life in such a way that it can legitimately take part in the reality of the common logos, in a genuine service of meaning. Out of such persons alone can circles be formed that follow the logos. These are they who genuinely think with one another because they genuinely talk to one another. All men, according to Heracleitus, have an essential share in self-knowledge and sensible thinking. That is naturally something that each person can only fulfil personally; but while they fulfil it and in so far as they fulfil it, they take part in the self-knowledge of man and in his common thinking. And again, no matter how numberless are the people of whom Heracleitus says that they understand neither how to listen nor how to talk, no aberration, no perversion of thought can undermine the fact that such communal guarding of meaning is existentially effected.

But there is also in the Heracleitian idea of the common cosmos an existential demand to be disclosed. The logos that becomes known as meaningful word between men is the same as that which immutably governs the swinging opposites of our cosmos. Indeed, without this lightninglike rudder, 'the most beautiful world order', according to Heracleitus, would be 'like a heap of chaotically spilled-out refuse'. But we ourselves too, as the ready and obedient bearers of the word of the logos, accord to the cosmos its reality which consists in being our world. Through us it becomes the shaped world of man, and only now does it deserve the name of cosmos as a total order, formed and revealed. Only through our service to the logos does the world become 'the same cosmos for all'. Thus and only thus do the waking, just in so far as they are awake, have in truth a single common world whose unity and community they work on in all real waking existence. For in sleep we are also, of course, as Heracleitus says, 'workers and co-workers' in the world happening, passive workers; but only awake, only working together awake, do we allow the totality of this happening to become manifest as cosmos. For then we experience with one another, help one another experience, and supplement one another in our experience: the living working together with the other living, and all the living with all the dead. 'Not as men asleep', says Heracleitus, 'must we act and speak.' For in sleep appearance reigns, but reality exists only in waking and, in fact, only to the degree of our working together. However, this working together is in no way to be conceived of as a team hitched to the great wagon; it is a strenuous tug of war for a wager, it is battle and strife. But in so far as it lets itself be determined by the logos it is a common battle and produces the common: out of the extremest tension, when it takes place in the service of the logos, arises ever anew the harmony of the lyre. Here the second existential demand of Heracleitus is comprehensible: that the person disengage himself from the great indolence, which Heracleitus calls a cowlike satiety, and that he realize in the common logos what is unique to him without curtailing its uniqueness, and that he work thereby on the common cosmos. This cosmos from which we come and which comes from us is, understood in its depth, infinitely greater than the sum of all special spheres of dreams and intoxication into which man flees before the demand of the We.

8

Heracleitus does not say 'We'. He would not have denied, nonetheless, that one cannot follow the logos more adequately than by saying 'We'—by saying it not frivolously and not impudently, but in truth. Since then the genuine saying of We has been manifest ever again in the way of life of the human race though also, of course, more and more endangered. What was and is said thereby is directly opposite to what Kierkegaard designates as the 'crowd'—opposite as the clear shape is to its caricature.

The genuine We is to be recognized in its objective existence, through the fact that in whatever of its parts it is regarded, an essential relation between person and person, between I and Thou, is always evident as actually or potentially existing. For the word always arises only between an I and a Thou, and the element from which the We receives its life is speech, the communal speaking that begins in the midst of speaking to one another.

Speech in its ontological sense was at all times present wherever men regarded one another in the mutuality of I and Thou; wherever one showed the other something in the world in such a way that from then on he began really to perceive it; wherever one gave another a sign in such a way that he could recognize the designated situation as he had not been able to before; wherever one communicated to the other his own experience in such a way that it penetrated the other's circle of experience and supplemented it as from within, so that from now on his perceptions were set within a world as they had not been before. All this flowing ever again into a great stream of reciprocal sharing of knowledge—thus came to be and thus is the living We, the genuine We, which, where it fulfils itself, embraces the dead who once took part in colloquy and now take part in it through what they have handed down to posterity.

The We of which I speak is no collective, no group, no objectively exhibitable multitude. It is related to the saying of 'We' as the I to the saying of 'I'. Just as little as the I does it allow itself to be carried over factually into the third person. But it does not have the comparative constancy and continuity that the I has. As potentiality it lies at the base of all history of spirit and deed; it actualizes itself and is no longer there. It can actualize itself within a group which then consists of just a fiery core and a drossy crust, and it can flare up and burn outside of all collectives. In the atmosphere of debates it cannot breathe, and no multitude of the so-called like-minded can legitimately say 'We' in the midst of debate; but it also happens even today that people are speaking in many tongues and suddenly the genuine We lives and moves in their speech.

Man has always had his experiences as I, his experiences with others, and with himself; but it is as We, ever again as We, that he has constructed and developed a world out of his experiences. A band, say of the same age, in which the overwhelming new experience had by the individuals becomes speech in animated shouting and immediately finds confirming and supplementing echo—a band and again a band; thus was originally obtained, I suppose, out of the abyss of being the common cosmos, the shaped order of what is experienced by man and what is known as experiencable, a shape that grows and changes. And thus also, in the midst of precipitous being, the human cosmos is preserved, guarded by its moulder, the human speech-with-meaning, the common logos. Thus the cosmos is preserved amid the changes of the world images.

Man has always thought his thoughts as I, and as I he has transplanted his ideas into the firmament of the spirit, but as We he has ever raised them into being itself, in just that mode of existence that I call 'the between' or 'betweenness'. That is the mode of existence between persons communicating with one another, which we cannot co-ordinate with either the psychic or the physical realms. It is to this that the seventh Platonic epistle points when it hints at the existence of a teaching which attains to effective reality not otherwise than in manifold togetherness and living with one another, as a light is kindled from leaping fire. Leaping fire is indeed the right image for the dynamic between persons in We.

The flight from the common cosmos into a special sphere that is understood as the true being is, in all its stages, from the elemental sayings of the ancient Eastern teachings to the arbitrariness of the modern counsel to intoxication, a flight from the existential claim on the person who must verify himself in We. It is flight from the authentic spokenness of speech in whose realm a response is demanded, and response is responsibility.

The fleeing man acts as if speech were nothing but the temptation to falsehood and convention, and it can, indeed, become temptation; but it is also our great pledge of truth.

For the typical man of today the flight from responsible personal existence has singularly polarized. Since he is not willing to answer for the genuineness of his existence, he flees either into the general collective which takes from him his responsibility or into the attitude of a self who has to account to no one but himself and finds the great general indulgence in the security of being identical with the Self of being. Even if this attitude is turned into a depeened contemplation of existing being, it remains a flight from the leaping fire.

The clearest mark of this kind of man is that he cannot really listen to the voice of another; in all his hearing, as in all his seeing, he mixes observation. The other is not the man over against him whose claim stands over against his own in equal right; the other is only his object. But he who existentially knows no Thou will never succeed in knowing a We.

In our age, in which the true meaning of every word is encompassed by delusion and falsehood, and the original intention of the human glance is stifled by tenacious mistrust, it is of decisive importance to find again the genuineness of speech and existence as We. This is no longer a matter which concerns the small circles that have been so important in the essential history of man; this is a matter of leavening the human race in all places with genuine We-ness. Man will not persist in existence if he does not learn anew to persist in it as a genuine We.

We had to confront the degenerate Western spirit with its origin and have therefore summoned the help of Heracleitus. But now he parts from us in our need or we part from him. For what he designates as the common has nothing that is over against it as such: logos and cosmos are, to him, self-contained; there is nothing that transcends them. And even when Heracleitus bears witness to the divine as at once bearing a name and being nameless, even then there is no real transcendence. No salvation is in sight for us, however, if we are not able again 'to stand before the face of God' in all reality as a We— as it is written in that faithful speech that once from Israel, the southern pillar of the bridge between the East and the West, started on its way.

In our age this We standing before the divine countenance has attained its highest expression through a poet, through Friedrich Hölderlin (1770-1843). He says of the authentic past of man as man, 'since we have been a dialogue and have been able to hear from one another'. And after that comes the words, 'But we are soon song'. The self-contained communality of Heracleitus that overspans the opposites has here become the choral antiphony which, as we know from Hölderlin, is directed upward.

CHAPTER V

THE WORD THAT IS SPOKEN[1]

1

If we proceed from the human life that each of us lives and the significance of the word for this life, then three modes-of-being of language are distinguishable. We shall call them present continuance, potential possession, and actual occurrence. By this is meant the continuance, possession, and occurrence at any given time of a certain language.

By present continuance is meant the totality of that which can be spoken in a particular realm of language in a particular segment of time, regarded from the point of view of the person who is able to say what is to be said. The place of this present continuance is, accordingly, the being-with-one-another of all the speakers of this realm of language, who again and again dispose of its existence in the language which they intend and which they utter, that is, the being-with-one-another of living men in whose personal texture of speech the present continuance becomes actualized. But this place of present continuance would be completely missed if one regarded the continuance as existing outside of these men. Every attempt to understand and to explain the present continuance of a language as accessible detached from the context of its actual speakers, must lead us astray.

By potential possession is meant the totality of what has ever been uttered in a certain realm of language, in so far as it proves itself capable of being included: included in what men

[1] Trans. by Maurice Friedman.

intend to utter and do utter. The possession legitimately extends, therefore, from the highest to the most trivial utterance. The place of possession is the sum of what in a language, up to a certain period of time, has been spoken and written in all its forms of preservation, with the decisive limitation, however, that nothing belongs to it except what can still today be lifted by a living speaker into the sphere of the living word, what can be brought home in it. No matter how fundamentally the philologist or the historian of literature can objectively apprehend it, even this mode-of-being of language, apparently unfolded in pure objectivity, cannot be detached in its dynamic facticity from the actuality of the word.

The third mode-of-being of language is that of its actual occurrence—its spokenness, or rather being spoken—the word that is spoken. The other two, existence and possession, presuppose an historical acquisition, but here nothing else is to be presupposed than man's will to communicate as a will capable of being realized. This will originates in men's turning to one another; it wins gesture, vocal sign, the word in the growing fruitfulness of this basic attitude. The elements of continuing language and the forms of possessed language serve it.

The genuine author and genuine dialogue—both draw from the present continuance of language, hence not from the dammed-up basin of possession, but from the gushing and streaming waters. The author, however, receives his creative force in fief from his partner in dialogue. Were there no more genuine dialogue, there would also be no more poetry. On the other hand, in the darkness of a world that has become spiritually unproductive, two whose call remains trustworthy can still, drawing from the present continuance of language, help each other ever again to say to each other what they have suffered in common.

What Goethe reports to us in a significant passage about the speech of heaven to earth in its primeval age: 'Wie das Wort so wichtig dort war, weil es ein gesprochen Wort war' ('How important the word was there, because it was a spoken word'), must also hold true within our human world. We can well believe Goethe. But what then lends this priority to the spoken word? Is not what we take from the present continuance of language in order to think it, or what we take from the possession of language in order to read it, often incalculably superior to the spoken word? The importance of the spoken word, I think, is grounded in the fact that it does not want to remain with the speaker. It reaches out toward a hearer, it lays hold of him, it even makes the hearer into a speaker, if perhaps only a soundless one. But this must not be understood as if the place of the occurrence of language is the sum of the two partners in dialogue or, in the terminology of Jakob Grimm, of the two 'fellows in speech'; as though the occurrence of language were to be understood through the psychophysical comprehension of two individual unities in a given period of time. The word that is spoken is found rather in the oscillating sphere between the persons, the sphere that I call 'the between' and that we can never allow to be contained without a remainder in the two participants. If we could take an inventory of all the physical and psychic phenomena to be found within a dialogical event, there would still remain outside something *sui generis* that could not be included—and that is just what does not allow itself to be understood as the sum of the speech of two or more speakers, together with all the accidental circumstances. This something *sui generis* is their dialogue.

We tend, to be sure, to forget that something can happen not merely 'to' us and 'in' us but also, in all reality, between us. Let us consider the most elementary of all facts of our intercourse with one another. The word that is spoken is uttered here and heard there, but its spokenness has its place in 'the between'.

2

Against the insight into the dialogical character of speech, it will probably be pointed out that thinking is essentially a man's speaking to himself. A reality is doubtless touched on here, but it is only touched on, not grasped. The so-called dialogue with oneself is possible only because of the basic fact of men's speaking with each other; it is the 'internalization' of this capacity. But he who does not shun the difficult task of reflecting on a past hour of his thinking—not according to its outcome, but fundamentally, according to its events, beginning with the beginning—may thrust inward to a primal level through which he can now wander without meeting a word. One notices that one has got hold of something without perceiving any conceptuality that wishes to come into being. In such a backward glance the second level allows itself to be seen more clearly, dominated by precisely this wishing to come into being. We may designate it as that of striving toward language. What is within strives over and over again toward becoming language, thought language, conceiving language. And only now in our work of memory do we enter into the true level of language. Here, indeed, language, even when still soundless, is already recognizably spoken. But does the thinker speak to himself as to the one thinking? In speaking the inner word he does not want to be heard by himself, for he knows it already as the person uttering it. Rather he wants to be heard by the nameless, unconceived, inconceivable other, by whom he wants to be understood in his having understood. The thinker is originally more solitary than the poet, but he is not more solitary in terms of his goal. Like the poet he is turned toward without turning himself. Certainly it is a court of his own through which he makes the competent examination of his world of concepts, but this world is not intended for this court, not dedicated to it. Many modern—and that means often de-Socratizing—philosophers have fallen, with the totality of their thought world, into a monologizing hubris, something which rarely happens to a poet. But this monologism, which, to be sure, is well acquainted with the existentialist but not with the existential, means in all its conjuring force the starkest menace of disintegration.

Every attempt to understand monologue as fully valid conversation, which leaves unclear whether it or dialogue is the more original, must run aground on the fact that the ontological basic presupposition of conversation is missing from it, the otherness, or more concretely, the moment of surprise. The human person is not in his own mind unpredictable to himself as he is to any one of his partners: therefore, he cannot be a genuine partner to himself, he can be no real questioner and no real answerer. He always 'already knows somewhere' the answer to the question, and not, to be sure, in the 'unconscious' of modern psychology, but rather in a sphere of conscious existence, a sphere which, although not present at the moment of the question, can in the very next moment flash up into presentness.

In philosophical discussions of language, speaking has occasionally been described as 'monadic' through and through'. This interpretation may not validly appeal to Wilhelm von Humboldt's givenness of the Thou in the I; for Humboldt knew exactly through what process the fact of the Thou in the I is established: through the I becoming a Thou to another I. 'From where else could the fundamental possibility of misunderstanding or being misunderstood originate?' asks the philosopher Hönigswald, mistakenly appealing to Humboldt in this connection. But what if precisely this possibility belongs essentially to speaking because language by its nature is a system of possible tensions—and thinking is just for this reason not a 'speaking with oneself' because it lacks the real tension? It is not true that a dialogue in which two speakers aim at an understanding of the meaning of an event must presuppose, as John Locke thought, an already existing understanding on the meaning of the words employed. When two friends discuss, say, the concept of thought, then the concept of the one and that of the other may be very similar in meaning; but we are not allowed to regard them as identical in meaning. This does not cease to be true even when the two of them begin by agreeing on a definition of the concept: the great fact of personal existence will penetrate even into the definition unless the two 'fellows in speech' join in betraying the logos for logical analysis. If the tension between what each means by the concept becomes too great, there arises a misunderstanding that can mount to destruction. But below the critical point the tension need by no means remain inoperative; it can become fruitful, it always becomes fruitful where, out of understanding each other, genuine dialogue unfolds.

From this it follows that it is not the unambiguity of a word but its ambiguity that constitutes living language. The ambiguity creates the problematic of speech, and it creates its overcoming in an understanding that is not an assimilation but a fruitfulness. The ambiguity of the word, which we may call

104

its aura, must to some measure already have existed whenever men in their multiplicity met each other, expressing this multiplicity in order not to succumb to it. It is the communal nature of the logos as at once 'word' and 'meaning' which makes man man, and it is this which proclaims itself from of old in the communalizing of the spoken word that again and again comes into being.

I recall how about forty-five years ago, I received from an International Institute for Philosophy in Amsterdam, at whose head stood the mathematician Brouwer, the plan of an academy whose task it should be 'to create words of spiritual value for the language of the western peoples', that is, words freed from ambiguity. I answered that in my judgment one should fight the misuse of the great old words rather than teach the use of new, manufactured ones. For in language, as in general, the *set* community kills the living. Certainly modern science has the great right to create for its purposes a medium of understanding that may be employed without remainder, but modern science knows that the word that is spoken can never arise in this way.

3

If, as we have seen, a monological primal character of language cannot be proved from the self-experience of thinking men, still less can it be discovered in the realm of phylogenesis. Certainly, it is an imperatively valid symbol when the Biblical narrative shows God as leaving to man the naming of the animals that He leads past him, but this happens to man as a being already standing in an adequate communication: it is through God's addressing man—Franz Rosenzweig's *Stern der Erlösung* teaches us—that He establishes man in speech. A precommunicative stage of language is unthinkable. Man did not exist before having a fellow being, before he lived over against him, toward him, and that means before he had dealings with him. Language never existed before address; it could become monologue only after dialogue broke off or broke down. The early speaker was not surrounded by objects on which he imposed names, nor did adventures befall him which he caught with names: the world and destiny became language for him only in partnership. Even when in a solitude beyond the range of call the hearerless word pressed on his throat, this word was connected with the primal possibility, that of being heard.

I will explain what I mean by an ethnological state of facts: by citing those remarkable word-compounds, adequately comprehensible to our thinking only as a residue of an early stage of language, which are preserved in the languages of many societies unrelated to one another—in particular those of the Eskimo and the Algonquin. In these so-called polysynthetic or holophrastic languages, the unit of speech with which one builds is not the word but the sentence. This is a structure that in its fully developed form exhibits components of three different kinds.[1] Two of them, the so-called core element and the formal elements both the modal as well as the personal, can also emerge as independent. Not so the element of the third kind, which might be designated as preponderantly suffixes: they appear exclusively in their serving function, but it is they that properly make possible the form of the sentence.

It would, to be sure, be presumptuous to connect our ideas about the origin of language with an attempted reconstruction of the genesis of that particular form of the sentence, but at any rate one is reminded of J. G. Hamann's bold statement that at first the word probably 'was neither a noun nor a verb but at the least a whole period'. We do not find as decisive man confronting things that he undertakes to put into words and only in this way bringing them to their full status as things. As important as this act is, we still find as decisive men with one another who undertake to come to an understanding over situations. Not things but situations are primary. If Stefan George's saying that no thing exists for which the word is wanting may hold true for things, it is inapplicable to the situations that man is given to know before he comes to know the things. Out of different situations of different kinds that early man experiences emerge similar, so to speak similar-remaining, things and beings, events and states that want to be conceived as such, named as such.

[1] I follow here almost throughout the formulation of Edward Sapir, without being able to go along with his general basic view.

In the early period, which we seek to disclose in this way, language presents itself to us above all as the manifestation and apprehension of an actual situation between two or more men who are bound together through a particular being-directed-to-each-other. This moment may, for example, be grounded in work in which the labour is shared, work in which the participants are often separated from each other, yet not so far that each is unable to hear clearly the articulated utterances of the other. If one man finds himself in a new, unforeseen situation, though not one unknown in its nature—for example, that of a threatening danger the like of which has already existed—then he calls to his comrade something that can be understood by the latter, but not by the members of an unfriendly neighbouring clan that might be in the vicinity. What I speak of is in no way to be compared with a 'cry for help' or a 'signal', as they are known to us from the life of animals, the first as improvised, the second as an utterance returning in unchanged form under similar circumstances. We can derive it from neither of the two, for even the most undifferentiated word designating a primordial situation must, just as a word, already have brought to sound that sudden and discovering freedom, alien to the animal, in which one man turns to the other in order to lead him to take notice of something existing or happening. Every genetic investigation which preserves its disinterestedness confirms for us the old insight which cannot be referred to often enough: that the mystery of the coming-to-be of language and that of the coming-to-be of man are one.

I have already drawn attention to the fact that the solitary category 'man' is to be understood as a working together of distance and relation (see pp. 59-71). Unlike all other living beings, man stands over against a world from which he has been set at a distance, and, unlike all other living beings, he can again and again enter into relationship with it. This fundamental double stance nowhere manifests itself so comprehensively as in language. Man—he alone—speaks, for only he can address the other just as the other being standing at a distance over against him; but in addressing it, he enters into relationship. The coming-to-be of language also means a new function of distance. For even the earliest speaking does not,

like a cry or a signal, have its end in itself; it sets the word
outside itself in being, and the word continues, it has continuance. And this continuance wins its life ever anew in true
relation, in the spokenness of the word. Genuine dialogue
witnesses to it, and poetry witnesses to it. For the poem is
spokenness, spokenness to the Thou, wherever this partner
might be.

But—so it may be asked—if this is so, if it is not a metaphor
but a fact that the poem is a spokenness, then does that not
necessarily mean that not merely the dialogue but also the
poem can be regarded according to its content of truth? This
question can only be answered with Yes and No at once. Every
authentic poem is also true, but its truth stands outside all
relation to an expressible What. We call poetry the not very
frequently appearing verbal form that imparts to us a truth
which cannot come to words in any other manner than just
in this one, in the manner of this form. Therefore, every
paraphrase of a poem robs it of its truth. I say, The poem
speaks; one may also say: The poet speaks—if one does not
mean by that the subject of a biography and the author of many
works, but just the living speaker of this very poem. The speaker
is as poet the speaker of a truth. Nietzsche's jest, 'The poets
lie too much', misses the depth of this truth, which is submerged
in the mystery of the witnessing How. Also bound up with
these facts is the problematic of the interpretation of poetry
in so far as it seeks anything further than that the word-
compound be more adequately perceived. The conceptuality
that sets as its goal bringing a knowable What to clarity and
value, diverts us from the genuine understanding of the poem
and misses the truth borne by it.

But if the name of truth really belongs to both, the conceptual
and the poetic, how can one lay hold of one truth that embraces
both? For a first answer to this question about the two truths
and the one, an ancient text which points to the primal phenomenon of language may help us.

A holy scripture of India, the Brahmana of the Hundred
Paths, relates that the gods and the demons both sprang from
the self-sacrifice of the primal creator and entered into his
heritage. Then it says:

The heritage, that was the word: truth and falsehood, at once truth and falsehood. Now this and that one spoke the truth, this and that one spoke the falsehood. Since they spoke the same, they were like one another. But now the gods rejected the falsehood and accepted the truth alone; but now the demons rejected the truth and accepted the falsehood alone. Then that truth that was with the demons pondered: 'Well, the gods have rejected the falsehood and have accepted the truth alone. So I shall go thither.' And it came to the gods. But that false-hood that was with the gods pondered: 'Well, the demons have rejected the truth and have accepted the falsehood alone. So I shall go thither.' And it went to the demons. Now the gods spoke the whole truth, the demons spoke the whole false-hood. Since the gods spoke only the truth, they became weaker and poorer, therefore, whoever speaks only the truth always becomes weaker and poorer. But in the end he endures, and in the end the gods endured. And the demons, who only spoke the falsehood, grew and thrived; therefore, whoever speaks only the falsehood grows and thrives. But in the end he cannot endure, and the demons could not endure.

It is worth noticing how here the fate of being is determined through the speaking of the word, and, indeed, through the speaking of the true and of the false word. But what can 'true' and 'false' mean to us when we transpose the myth into our human reality? Clearly not something that can be grasped only through the relation to a reality existing outside the speaking. The myth knows only the totality of the one, still undivided sphere. When we shift from the myth into our world, therefore, we can turn toward no other sphere commensurate with that one. 'One speaks the truth' may, accordingly, be paraphrased by: 'One says what he means.' But what meaning does 'mean' have here? In our world and in our language this obviously signifies that just as the speaker, because he is who he is, means what he means, so also because he is who he is, he says what he means. The relation between meaning and saying points us to the relation between the intended unity of meaning and saying, on the one side, and that between meaning and saying and the personal existence itself, on the other side.

In this myth an especially strong accent falls on the establish-ment of the fact that—expressed in our language—the truth, chemically purified, as it were of its content of falsehood, is ineffectual in the course of history. Everything depends here on interpreting correctly the words, 'But in the end he endures'. This is no expression of an optimistic view of history, nor is it an eschatological saying. 'In the end' means for us: in the pure reckoning of the personal existence. In the language of religion it is expressed thus: 'When the books are opened'; that is not there and then, however, but here and now.

The truth that is concerned in this fashion is not the sublime 'unconcealment' suitable to Being itself, the *aletheia* of the Greeks; it is the simple conception of truth of the Hebrew Bible, whose *etymon* means 'faithfulness', the faithfulness of man or the faithfulness of God. The truth of the word that is genuinely spoken is, in its highest forms—in poetry and incomparably still more so in that messagelike saying that descends out of the stillness over a disintegrating human world —indivisible unity. It is a manifestation without a concomitant diversity of aspects. In all its other forms, however, three different elements must be distinguished in it. It is, in the first place, faithful truth in relation to the reality which was once perceived and is now expressed, to which it opens wide the window of language in order that it may become directly perceptible to the hearer. It is, second, faithful truth in relation to the person addressed, whom the speaker means as such, no matter whether he bears a name or is anonymous, is familiar or alien. And to mean a man means nothing less than to stand by him and his insight with the elements of the soul that can be sent forth, with the 'outer soul', even though at the same time one fundamentally remains and must remain with oneself. Third, it is the truth of the word that is genuinely spoken, faithful truth in relation to its speaker, that is, to his factual existence in all its hidden structure. The human truth of which I speak—the truth vouchsafed men—is no pneuma that pours itself out from above on a band of men now become super-personal: it opens itself to one just in one's existence as a person. This concrete person, in the life-space allotted to him, answers with his faithfulness for the word that is spoken by him.

CHAPTER VI

GUILT AND GUILT FEELINGS[1]

―――――

1

At the London International Conference for Medical Psychotherapy of 1948,[2] 'The Genesis of Guilt' was fixed as the theme
of the first plenary session. The first speaker, a Hollander,
began with the announcement that in his special group the
question had been discussed as to whether the genesis of guilt
or the genesis of guilt feelings was meant. The question
remained unclarified. But in the course of the discussion it was
left to the theologians to speak of guilt itself (by which, indeed,
they did not actually mean personal guilt, but the original sin
of the human race). The psychologists concerned themselves
merely with guilt feelings.

This distribution of themes, through which the factual
occurrences of guilt in the lives of 'patients', of suffering men,
hardly enters into view, is characteristic of most of what one
calls the psychotherapeutic discipline. Only in the most recent
period have some begun to complain that both in the theory and
in the practice of this science the psychic 'projection' of guilt is
afforded room, the real events of guilt are not. This omission
has not been been presented and methodologically grounded
as such. It has been treated as a limitation that follows as a
matter of course from the nature of psychology.

Nothing of the kind is self-evident, however; indeed, nothing
of the kind by right exists. Certainly, in the course of the history

―――――

[1] Trans. by Maurice Friedman.
[2] International Congress of Mental Health, London 1948; *Proceedings of the
International Conference on Medical Psychotherapy*, Vol. III.

of the spirit each science that has detached itself from a comprehensive context and ensured for itself the independence of
its realm has just thereby severely and ever more severely
limited its subject and the manner of its working. But the
investigator cannot truthfully maintain his relationship with
reality—a relationship without which all his work becomes a
well-regulated game—if he does not again and again, whenever
it is necessary, gaze beyond the limits into a sphere which is
not his sphere of work, yet which he must contemplate with all
his power of research in order to do justice to his own task. For
the psychotherapist this sphere is formed from the factual
course of the so-called external life of his patients and especially
the actions and attitudes therein, and again especially the
patient's active share in the manifold relation between him and
the human world. Not only his decisions are included in this
share, but also his failures to come to a decision when, in a
manner perceptible to him, they operate as decisions.

To the valid scientific realm of psychotherapy belong the
'inner' reactions of the individual to his passive and active
life-experience, the psychic elaboration of the biographical
events, whether it takes place in conscious or in unconscious
processes. The relationship of the patient to a man with whom
he stands in a contact that strongly affects his own life is for
the psychologist important as such only in so far as its effects
on the psyche of the patient can serve the understanding of his
illness. The relationship itself in its reciprocal reality, the
significant actuality of what is happening and has happened
between the two men, transcends his task as it transcends his
method. He limits himself to those of its inner connections that
his work of exploring the mind of the patient makes accessible
to him. And yet, if he wishes to satisfy not merely what he
owes to the laws of his discipline and their application, but also
what he owes to the existence and the need of man, he may, in
fact he must, go beyond that realm where an existing person
merely relates to himself. He must cast his glance again and
again to where existing person relates to existing person—
this person, the 'patient', to another living being who is not
'given' to the doctor and who may be completely unknown to
him. The psychotherapist cannot include this other person,

these other persons in his work. It is not for him to concern himself with them. And yet he may not neglect them in their reality; he must succeed in grasping their reality as adequately as possible in so far as it enters into the relationship between them and his patient.

This state of affairs manifests itself with the greatest intensity in the problem that occupies us here. Within his methods the psychotherapist has to do only with guilt feelings, conscious and unconscious (Freud was already aware of the contradiction that lies in the concept of unconscious feelings). But within a comprehensive service to knowledge and help, he must himself encounter guilt as something of an ontic character whose place is not the soul but being. He will do this, to be sure, with the danger that through his new knowledge the help which he is obliged to give might also be modified so that something uncustomary will be demanded of his method; indeed, he must be ready even to step out of the established rules of his school. But a 'doctor of souls' who really is one—that is, who does not merely carry on the work of healing but enters into it at times as a partner—is precisely one who dares.

2

The boundaries set by the psychotherapist's method do not, in any case, suffice to explain the negative or indifferent attitude that psychotherapy has so long taken toward the ontic character of guilt. The history of modern psychology shows us that here deeper motives are at work that have also contributed to the genesis and development of the methods. The two clearest examples of it are provided us by the two most note-worthy representatives of this intellectual tendency: Freud and Jung.

Freud, a great, late-born apostle of the enlightenment, presented the naturalism[1] of the enlightenment with a scientific system and thereby with a second flowering. As Freud himself

---

[1] Freud himself described psychoanalysts as 'incorrigible mechanists and materialists' (Sigmund Freud, 'Psycho-analysis and Telepathy', in *The Standard Edition of the Complete Psychological Works of Sigmund Freud*, XVIII (London: Hogarth Press, 1955), pp. 177–193.

recognized with complete clarity,[1] the struggle against all metaphysical and religious teachings of the existence of an absolute and of the possibility of a relation of the human person to it had a great share in the development of psychoanalytic theory. As a result of this basic attitude, guilt was simply not allowed to acquire an ontic character; it had to be derived from the transgression against ancient and modern taboos, against parental and social tribunals. The feeling of guilt was now to be understood as essentially only the consequence of dread of punishment and censure by this tribunal, as the consequence of the child's fear of 'loss of love' or, at times when it was a question of imaginary guilt, as a 'need for punishment' of a libidinal nature, as 'moral masochism'[2] which is complemented by the sadism of the superego. 'The first renunciation of instinctual gratification', Freud stated in 1924, 'is enforced by external powers, and it is this that creates morality which expresses itself in conscience and exacts a further renunciation of instinct.'[3]

Of an entirely different, indeed diametrically opposed, nature is the teaching of Carl Jung, whom one can describe as a mystic of a modern, psychological type of solipsism. The mystical and religio-mystical conceptions that Freud despised are for Jung the most important subject of his study; but they are such merely as 'projections' of the psyche, not as indications of something extrapsychic that the psyche meets. For Freud the structure of the psyche culminates in the superego, which represents, with its censory function, only the authoritative tribunals of family and society; for Jung it culminates or rather is grounded in the self, which is 'individuality in its highest meaning'[4] and forms 'the most immediate experience of the divine which can be grasped at all psychologically'.[5] Jung does not recognize at all any relationship between the individual

[1] See, for example, 'A Philosophy of Life', ch. 7 in Freud, *New Introductory Lectures on Psycho-Analysis* (London: Hogarth Press; New York: W. W. Norton, 1933).

[2] Freud, 'The Economic Problem in Masochism', in *Collected Papers* (London: Hogarth Press, 1948), pp. 255–268.

[3] *Ibid.*, p. 267.

[4] Carl Jung, *Von den Wurzeln des Bewusstseins*, Psychologische Abhandlungen, IX (Zurich: Rascher, 1954), pp. 296 f.

[5] *Ibid.*, p. 300.

soul and another existing being which oversteps the limits of the psychic. But to this must be added the fact that the integration of evil as the unification of the opposites in the psyche is put forward as a central motif in the process of 'individuation', of the 'realization of self'.[1] Seen from this vantage point, there is in Jung's panpsychism, as in Freud's materialism, no place for guilt in the ontological sense, unless it be in the relationship of man to himself—that is, as failure in the process of individuation. In fact, in the whole great work of Jung we learn nothing of guilt as a reality in the relation between the human person and the world entrusted to him in his life.

With the other psychoanalytic doctrines it stands, in general, much the same. Almost everyone who seriously concerns himself with the problem of guilt proceeds to derive the guilt feelings that are met with in analysis from hidden elements, to trace them back to such elements, to unmask them as such. One seeks the powerful repressions in the unconscious as those that hide behind the phenomena of illness, but not also the live connection the image of which has remained in the living memory, time and again admonishing, attacking, tormenting, and, after each submersion in the river of no-longer-thinking-about-that, returning and taking up its work anew.

A man stands before us who, through acting or failing to act, has burdened himself with a guilt or has taken part in a community guilt, and now, after years or decades is again and again visited by the memory of his guilt. Nothing of the genesis of his illness is concealed from him if he is only willing no longer to conceal from himself the guilt character of that active or passive occurrence. What takes possession of him ever again has nothing to do with any parental or social reprimand, and if he does not have to fear an earthly retribution and does not believe in a heavenly one, no court, no punishing power exists that can make him anxious. Here rules the one penetrating insight—the one insight capable of penetrating into the impossibility of recovering the original point of departure and the

[1] Carl Jung, *Von der Wurzeln des Bewusstseins*, Psychologische Abhandlungen, IX (Zurich: Rascher, 1954). For a fuller analysis of Jung, see Martin Buber, *Eclipse of God*, Section 2, 'Religion and Modern Thinking', and 'Supplement: Reply to C. G. Jung', trans. by Maurice Friedman.

irreparability of what has been done, and that means the real insight into the irreversibility of lived time, a fact that shows itself unmistakably in the starkest of all human perspectives, that concerning one's own death. From no standpoint is time perceived so like a torrent as from the vision of the self in guilt. Swept along in this torrent, the bearer of guilt is visited by the shudder of identity with himself. I, he comes to know, I, who have become another, am the same.

I have seen three important and, to me, dear men fall into long illnesses from their failing to stand the test in the days of an acute community guilt. The share of the psychogenic element in the illness could hardly be estimated, but its action was unmistakable. One of them refused to acknowledge his self-contradiction before the court of his spirit. The second resisted recognizing as serious a slight error he remembered that was attached to a very serious chain of circumstances. The third, however, would not let himself be forgiven by God for the blunder of a moment because he did not forgive himself. It now seems to me that all three needed and lacked competent helpers.

The psychotherapist into whose field of vision such manifestations of guilt enter in all their forcefulness can no longer imagine that he is able to do justice to his task as doctor of guilt-ridden men merely through the removal of guilt feelings. Here a limit is set to the tendency to derive guilt from the taboos of primeval society. The psychologist who sees what is here to be seen must be struck by the idea that guilt does not exist because a taboo exists to which one fails to give obedience, but rather that taboo and the placing of taboo have been made possible only through the fact that the leaders of early communities knew and made use of a primal fact of man as man—the fact that man can become guilty and know it.

Existential guilt—that is, guilt that a person has taken on himself as a person and in a personal situation—cannot be comprehended through such categories of analytical science as 'repression' and 'becoming conscious'. The bearer of guilt of whom I speak remembers it again and again by himself and in sufficient measure. Not seldom, certainly, he attempts to evade it—not the remembered fact, however, but its depths as existential guilt—until the truth of this depth overwhelms him and time is now perceived by him as a torrent.

Can the doctor of souls function here as helper, beyond professional custom and correct methods? May he do so? Is he shown at times another and higher therapeutic goal than the familiar one? Can and may he try his strength, not with conscious or unconscious, founded or unfounded guilt feelings, but with the self-manifesting existential guilt itself? Can he allow himself to recognize, from this standpoint, that healing in this case means something other than the customary, and what it means in this case?

The doctor who confronts the effects on the guilty man of an existential guilt must proceed in all seriousness from the situation in which the act of guilt has taken place. Existential guilt occurs when someone injures an order of the human world whose foundations he knows and recognizes as those of his own existence and of all common human existence. The doctor who confronts such a guilt in the living memory of his patient must enter into that situation; he must lay his hand in the wound of the order and learn: this concerns you. But then it may strike him that the orientation of the psychologist and the treatment of the therapist have changed unawares and that if he wishes to persist as a healer he must take upon himself a burden he had not expected to bear.

One could protest that an existential guilt is only the exception and that it is not proper to frighten the already overburdened therapist with the image of such borderline cases. But what I call existential guilt is only an intensification of what is found in some measure wherever an authentic guilt feeling burns, and the authentic guilt feeling is very often inextricably mingled with the problematic, the 'neurotic', the 'groundless'. The therapist's methods, naturally, do not willingly concern themselves with the authentic guilt feeling which, in general, is of a strictly personal character and does not easily allow itself to be imprisoned in general propositions. It lies essentially nearer to the doctrine and practice to occupy itself with the effects of repressed childhood wishes or youthful lusts gone astray, than with the inner consequences of a man's betrayal of his friend or his cause. And for the patient it is a great relief to be diverted from his authentic guilt feeling to an unambiguous neurotic one that, favoured within this category by the school of his doctor, allows itself to be discovered in the microcosmos of his dreams or in the stream of his free associations. To all this the genuine doctor of souls stands opposed with the postulative awareness that he should act here as at once bound and unbound. He does not, of course, desist from any of his methods, which have in fact become adaptable. But where, as here, he becomes aware of a reality between man and man, between man and the world, a reality inaccessible to any of the psychological categories, he recognizes the limits that are set here for his methods and recognizes that the goal of healing has been transformed in this case because the context of the sickness, the place of the sickness in being, has been transformed. If the therapist recognizes this, then all that he is obliged to do becomes more difficult, much more difficult—and all becomes more real, radically real.

3

I shall clarify this statement through the example of a life history that I have already made use of before, although all too briefly.[1] I select it from among those at my disposal because I was a witness, sometimes more distant, sometimes nearer, to the happenings, and I have followed their sequence. The life course I have in mind is that of a woman—let us call her Melanie—of more intellectual than truly spiritual gifts, with a scientific education, but without the capacity for independent mastery of her knowledge. Melanie possessed a remarkable talent for good comradeship which expressed itself, at least from her side, in more or less erotically tinged friendships that left unsatisfied her impetuous rather than passionate need for love. She made the acquaintance of a man who was on the point of marriage with another, strikingly ugly, but remarkable women. Melanie succeeded without difficulty in breaking up the

[1] See my Preface to Hans Trüb's posthumous work, *Heilung aus der Begegnung: Eine Auseinandersetzung mit der Psychologic C. G. Jungs*, ed. by Ernst Michel and Arie Sborowitz (Stuttgart: Ernst Klett Verlag, 1952). This Preface appears in English as 'Healing through Meeting' in Martin Buber, *Pointing the Way*, pp. 93–97.

engagement and marrying the man. Her rival tried to kill herself. Melanie soon afterwards accused her, certainly unjustly, of feigning her attempt at suicide. After a few years Melanie herself was supplanted by another woman. Soon Melanie fell ill with a neurosis linked with disturbances of the vision. To friends who took her in at the time, she confessed her guilt without glossing over the fact that it had arisen not out of a passion, but out of a fixed will.

Later she gave herself into the care of a well-known psycho-analyst. This man was able to liberate her in a short while from her feelings of disappointment and guilt and to bring her to the conviction that she was a 'genius of friendship' and would find in this sphere the compensation that was due her. The conversion succeeded, and Melanie devoted herself to a rich sociality which she experienced as a world of friendship. In contrast to this, she associated in general with the men with whom she had to deal in her professional 'welfare work' not as persons needing her understanding and even her consolation, but as objects to be seen through and directed by her. The guilt feelings were no longer in evidence; the apparatus that had been installed in place of the paining and admonishing heart functioned in model fashion.

Now that is certainly no extraordinary fate. We recognize again the all too usual distress of human action and suffering, and there can be no talk here of existential guilt in the great sense of the term. And yet, the guilt feeling that grew up at that time in the illness and that so fused with the illness that no one could say which of the two was the cause and which the effect, had throughout an authentic character. With the silencing of the guilt feeling there disappeared for Melanie the possibility of reconciliation through a newly won genuine relationship to her environment in which her best qualities could at the same time unfold. The price paid for the annihilation of the sting was the final annihilation of the chance to become the being that this created person was destined to become through her highest disposition.

Again one may raise the objection that it cannot be the affair of the psychotherapist to concern himself about this kind of thing. His task is to investigate malady and to heal it, or rather to help it toward healing, and it is just this that the doctor who had been called in had done. But here lies an important problem. Stated generally, one can formulate it somewhat as follows: Shall a man who is called upon to help another in a specific manner merely give the help for which he is summoned or shall he also give the other help that, according to the doctor's knowledge of him, this man objectively needs?

However, what is the meaning here of the help that one objectively needs? Clearly this, that his being follows other laws than his consciousness. But also quite other ones than his 'unconscious'. The unconscious is still far less concerned than the conscious about whether the essence of this man thrives. Essence—by this I mean that for which a person is peculiarly intended, what he is called to become. The conscious, with its planning and its weighing, concerns itself with it only occasionally; the unconscious, with its wishes and contradictions, hardly ever. Those are great moments of existence when a man discovers his essence or rediscovers it on a higher plane; when he decides and decides anew to become what he is and, as one who is becoming this, to establish a genuine relation to the world; when he heroically maintains his discovery and decision against his everyday consciousness and against his unconscious. Should the helper, can the helper, may the helper now enter into an alliance with the essence of him who summoned him, across this person's conscious and unconscious will, provided that he has really reliably recognized the need of this essence? Is something of this sort at all his office? Can it be his office? Particularly where the helping profession is so exactly circumscribed by principles and methods as in modern psychotherapy? Does not the danger threaten here of a pseudo-intuitive dilettantism that dissolves all fixed norms?

An important psychologist and doctor of our time, the late Viktor von Weizsaecker, laid down, in very precise language, a sober admonition on this point. There the 'treatment of the essential in man' is simply excluded from the realm of psychotherapy. 'Just the final destiny of man', he writes, 'must not be the subject of therapy.'[1] And my lay insight must concur with this declaration. But there is an exceptional case—the case

---

[1] *Herztliche-Fragen* (1934), p. 9.

where the glance of the doctor, the perceiving glance that makes him a doctor and to whom all his methods stand in a serving relation, extends into the sphere of the essence, where he perceives essential lapse and essential need. There, to be sure, it is still denied him to treat 'the essential' in his patients, but he may and should guide it to where an essential help of the self, a help till now neither willed nor anticipated, can begin. It is neither given the therapist nor allowed to him to indicate a way that leads onward from here. But from the watchtower to which the patient has been conducted, he can manage to see a way that is right for him and that he can walk, a way that it is not granted the doctor to see. For at this high station all becomes personal in the strictest sense.

The psychotherapist is no pastor of souls and no substitute for one. It is never his task to mediate a salvation; his task is always only to further a healing. But it is not merely incumbent upon him to interest himself in that need of the patient which has become symptomatically manifest in his sickness—to interest himself in it as far as the analysis conducted according to the therapist's method discloses to him the genesis of this illness. That need is also confided to him which first allows itself to be recognized in the immediacy of the partnership between the patient who is having recourse to the doctor and the doctor who is concerned about the recovery of the patient —although occasionally this need remains veiled, even then.

I have already pointed to the fact that the doctor, in order to be able to do this adequately, must for the time being lift himself off the firm ground of principles and methods on which he has learned to walk. One must not, of course, understand this to mean that he now soars in the free ether of an unrestrained 'intuition'. Now too, and only now really, he is obliged to think consistently and to work exactly. And if he may now surrender himself to a more direct vision, it can still only be one that realizes its individual norms in each of its insights—norms that cannot be translated into general propositions. In this sphere of action, too, even though it seems left to his independent direction, the man of the intellectual profession learns that a true work is an affair of a listening obedience.

121

But in order that the therapist be able to do this, he must recognize just one thing steadfastly and recognize it ever again: there exists real guilt, fundamentally different from all the anxiety-induced bugbears that are generated in the cavern of the unconscious. Personal guilt, whose reality some schools of psychoanalysis contest and others ignore, does not permit itself to be reduced to the trespass against a powerful taboo.

We cannot now content ourselves, however, with allowing this knowledge, which was long under a ban, to be conveyed to us by this or that tradition which is holy to us. It must arise anew from the historical and biographical self-experience of the generation living today. We who are living today know in what measure we have become historically and biographically guilty. That is no feeling and no sum of feelings. It is, no matter how manifoldly concealed and denied, a real knowledge about a reality. Under the schooling of this knowledge, which is becoming ever more irresistible, we learn anew that guilt exists.

In order to understand this properly we must call to mind one fact, no accessory fact but the basic one. Each man stands in an objective relationship to others; the totality of this relationship constitutes his life as one that factuality participates in the being of the world. It is this relationship, in fact, that first makes it at all possible for him to expand his environment (*Umwelt*) into a world (*Welt*). It is his share in the human order of being, the share for which he bears responsibility. An objective relationship in which two men stand to one another can rise, by means of the existential participation of the two, to a personal relation; it can be merely tolerated; it can be neglected; it can be injured. Injuring a relationship means that at this place the human order of being is injured. No one other than he who inflicted the wound can heal it. He who knows the fact of his guilt and is a helper can help him try to heal the wound.

4

One last clarification is still necessary. When the therapist recognizes an existential guilt of his patient, he cannot—that we have seen—show him the way to the world, which the latter must rather seek and find as his own personal law. The doctor can only conduct him to the point from which he can glimpse his personal way or at least its beginning. But in order that the doctor shall be able to do this, he must also know about the general nature of the way, common to all great acts of conscience, and about the connection that exists between the nature of existential guilt and the nature of this way.

In order not to fall into any error here, however, we must bear in mind that there are three different spheres in which the reconciliation of guilt can fulfil itself and between which noteworthy relations often establish themselves. Only one of these spheres, that which we shall designate as the middle one, directly concerns the therapist whom I have in mind.

The first sphere is that of the law of the society. The action begins here with the demand, actually made or latent, which society places on the guilty man according to its laws. The event of fulfilment is called confession of guilt. It is followed by penalty and indemnification. With this sphere the therapist, naturally, has nothing to do. As doctor, an opinion is not even accorded him as to whether the demand of the society is right or not. His patient, the guilty man, may be guilty toward the society or he may not be; its judgment over him may be just or it may not be. This does not concern the doctor as doctor; he is incompetent here. In his relation to the patient this problematic theme can find no admission, with the exception of the unavoidable occupation with the anxiety of the patient in the face of the punishments, the censure, the boycotts of society.

But the third and highest sphere, that of faith, also cannot be his affair. Here the action commences within the relation between the guilty man and his God and remains therein. It is likewise consummated in three events which correspond to the three of the first sphere, but are connected with each other in an entirely different manner. These are the confession of sin, repentence, and penance in its various forms. The doctor as such may not touch on this sphere even when he and the patient stand in the same community of faith. Here no man can speak unless it be one whom the guilty man acknowledges as a hearer and speaker who represents the transcendence believed in by the guilty man. Also when the therapist encounters the problem

123

of faith in the anxiety concerning divine punishment that is disclosed in the patient's analysis, he cannot interfere here— even if he possesses great spiritual gifts—without falling into a dangerous dilettantism.

The middle sphere, as we have said, is one to the sight of which the therapist may lead—up to it, but no farther. This sphere, about which he must *know* for this purpose, we may call that of conscience, with a qualification which I shall shortly discuss. The action demanded by the conscience also fulfils itself in three events, which I call self-illumination, perseverance, and reconciliation, and which I shall define more exactly still.

Conscience means to us the capacity and tendency of man radically to distinguish between those of his past and future actions which should be approved and those which should be disapproved. The disapproval, in general, receives far stronger emotional stress, whereas the approval of past actions at times passes over with shocking ease into a most questionable self-satisfaction. Conscience can, naturally, distinguish and if necessary condemn in such a manner not merely deeds but also omissions, not merely decisions but also failures to decide, indeed even images and wishes that have just arisen or are remembered.

In order to understand this capacity and tendency more exactly, one must bear in mind that among all living beings known to us man alone is able to set at a distance not only his environment (see pp. 60–68), but also himself. As a result, he becomes for himself a detached object about which he can not only 'reflect', but which he can, from time to time, confirm as well as condemn. The content of conscience is in many ways determined, of course, by the commands and prohibitions of the society to which its bearer belongs or those of the tradition of faith to which he is bound. But conscience itself cannot be understood as an introjection of either the one authority or the other, neither ontogenetically nor phylogenetically. The table of shalts and shalt-nots under which this man has grown up and lives determines only the conceptions which prevail in the realm of the conscience, but not its existence itself, which is grounded in just that distancing and distinguishing—primal qualities of the human race. The more or less hidden criteria that the conscience employs in its acceptances and rejections only rarely fully coincide with a standard received from the society or community. Connected with that is the fact that the guilt feeling can hardly ever be wholly traced to a transgression against a taboo of a family or of society. The totality of the order that a man knows to be injured or injurable by him transcends to some degree the totality of the parental and social taboos that bind him. The depth of the guilt feeling is not seldom connected with just that part of the guilt that cannot be ascribed to the taboo-offence, hence with the existential guilt.

The qualification of which I spoke, accordingly, is that our subject is the relation of the conscience to existential guilt. Its relation to the trespassing of taboos concerns us here only in so far as a guilty man understands this trespassing more strongly or weakly as real existential guilt which arises out of his being and for which he cannot take responsibility without being responsible to his relationship to his own being.

The vulgar conscience that knows admirably well how to torment and harass, but cannot arrive at the ground and abyss of guilt, is incapable, to be sure, of summoning to such responsibility. For this summoning a greater conscience is needed, one that has become wholly personal, one that does not shy away from the glance into the depths and that already in admonishing envisages the way that leads across it. But this in no way means that this personal conscience is reserved for some type of 'higher' man. This conscience is possessed by every simple man who gathers himself into himself in order to venture the breakthrough out of the entanglement in guilt. And it is a great, not yet sufficiently recognized, task of education to elevate the conscience from its lower common form to conscience-vision and conscience-courage. For it is innate to the conscience of man that it can elevate itself.

From what has been said it already follows with sufficient clarity that the primeval concept of conscience, if only it is understood as a dynamic one rather than as a static, judging one, is more realistic than the modern structural concept of the superego. The concept of the superego attains only an orienting significance and one, moreover, which easily orients the novice falsely.

If we now wish to speak of actions in the sphere of conscience in this high and strict sense, we do not mean thereby the well-known synthesis out of the internalization of censure, torment, and punishment that one customarily regards as the proper factual content of conscience—that pressuring and oppressing influence of an inner high court on an 'ego' that is more or less subject to it. Rather this tormenting complex has, for our consideration, only the character of an angelic–demonic intermezzo on which the high dramatic or tragicomic act of neurosis may follow, and the whole affair may end with a therapy that passes for successful. What concerns us here is another possibility, whether it be the true process of healing after the neurosis, or whether it be without a neurosis preceding it. It is that possible moment when the whole person who has become awake and unafraid ascends from the anguishing lowland of the conscience to its heights and independently masters the material delivered to him by it.

From this position a man can undertake the threefold action to which I have referred: first, to illuminate the darkness that still weaves itself about the guilt despite all previous action of the conscience—not to illuminate it with spotlights but with a broad and enduring wave of light; second, to persevere, no matter how high he may have ascended in his present life above that station of guilt—to persevere in that newly won humble knowledge of the identity of the present person with the person of that time; and third, in his place and according to his capacity, in the given historical and biographical situations, to restore the order-of-being injured by him through the relation of an active devotion to the world—for the wounds of the order-of-being can be healed in infinitely many other places than those at which they were inflicted.

In order that this may succeed in that measure that is at all attainable by this man, he must gather the forces and elements of his being and ever again protect the unity that is thus won from the cleavage and contradiction that threaten it. For, to quote myself, one cannot do evil with his whole soul, one can do good only with the whole soul.[1] What one must wrest from himself, first, is not yet the good; only when he has first attained his own self does the good thrive through him.

[1] Martin Buber, *Good and Evil: Two Interpretations* (New York: Charles Scribner's Sons, paperback, 1961), p. 130. British edition, *Images of Good and Evil* (London: Routledge, 1952).

5

The event of illumination corresponds on the plane of the law to the legal confession of guilt, on the plane of faith to the confession of sin. As a social concept, confession of guilt is naturally the most familiar of the three; what takes place here takes place in public in the legal institutions of society.

The confession of sin is spoken by a man when, seeking reconciliation with God, he directly or indirectly steps before the absolute judgment. That may happen in the chorus of the community, as at the Jewish Day of Atonement, or in the whispers of the confessing man into the ear of the confessor, or even in solitude by those who feel themselves as standing before God and their speech as addressing God: the confessing one is always removed from the anonymous publicity of society, but by no means referred to himself. He has one over against him who receives his confession, answers it, 'forgives' him— for the Jews, in a significant co-operation with him toward whom the confessing one has become guilty.

The matter is otherwise with the first of the three events in the action of the great conscience, the event of illumination. Here a man ventures to illuminate the depths of a guilt which he has certainly recognized as what it is, but not yet in its essence and its meaning for his life. What he is now obliged to do cannot be accomplished in any other place than in the abyss of I-with-me, and it is just this abyss that must be illuminated.

Legal confession of guilt means a dialogue with the representatives of society who rejoin as judges according to the penal law. Religious confession means a dialogue with the absolute divine person who replies in mysterious fashion out of his mystery. As for the illumination of essence, it is in its most real moments not even a monologue, much less a real conversation between an ego and a superego: all speech is exhausted; what takes place here is the mute shudder of self-being. But without this powerful wave of light which illuminates the abyss of mortality, the legal confession of guilt remains without substance in the inner life of the guilty man, no matter how weighty its consequences may be, and the religious confession is only a pathetic prattle that no one hears.

We must not fail to recognize that it has become more difficult for the man of our age than any earlier one to venture self-illumination with awake and unafraid spirit, although he imagines that he knows more about himself than did the man of any earlier time. The inner resistance which shows itself here—a deeper one than all that discloses itself to the genetic investigation of the analyst—has found so valid a representation in two of the characteristic forms of the epic literatures of the nineteenth and twentieth centuries that we cannot do better than to turn to them in order to supplement our understanding of the problem. I mean Nikolai Stavrogin in Dostoevski's novel *The Possessed* and Joseph K in Kafka's narrative *The Trial*. In our discussion of this subject, the second of these books, as little as it is comparable to the first in artistic power, must still be the more important because in it the present stage of the human problem of guilt has found expression. But in order to see how this later stage is connected with that which preceded it, we must turn our attention first to Dostoevski.

For our formulation of the question it is necessary to proceed from the complete text of the novel, that which contains the chapter of Stavrogin's confession, later expunged by the author on external grounds, and some related material.

Stavrogin was thought of by Dostoevski as the man on the outermost rim of the age who dissolves the meaning of existence through denying it and who manages to destroy himself through the destruction of all over whom he gets power. In the omitted chapter it is told how Stavrogin visits a holy man and brings to him the record of a confession which he declares he wishes to publish. In it he confesses how he raped a little girl. Later he disavows the confession, evidently because he knows from the reaction of the priest as soon as it has been made that it cannot accomplish what he has expected it to. The content of the confession is true, but the act of making it is fictitious. It has nothing at all to do with Stavrogin's self-illumination, with persevering self-identification, with reconciling renewed relationship with the world. Thus even his 'unfeigned need for a public execution' (as Dostoevski states in explanation) is permeated with the fictitious. What Stavrogin desires is 'the leap'. A fragmentary sketch by Dostoevski informs us unambiguously about this. It says, clearly in this connection, that the priest opposed Stavrogin's intention to publish the confession: 'The high priest pointed out that a leap was not necessary, that the man must rather set himself to rights from within—through long work; only then could he complete the leap. "And would it be impossible to do it suddenly?" Stavrogin asks. "Impossible?" rejoins the priest. "From the work of an angel it would become the work of a devil." "Ah," exclaims Stavrogin, "that I already knew myself."'

Stavrogin 'commits' the confession as he commits his crimes: as an attempt to snatch the genuine existence which he does not possess, but which—nihilist in practice but (in anticipation) existentialist in views—he has recognized as the true good. He is full of 'ideas' (Dostoevski even lends him his own!), full of 'spirit', but he does not exist. Only after Dostoevski's time, only in our own, will this type of man discover the basic nihilism in existential form after he has learned that he cannot attain to existence by the ways corresponding to his kind of person. Only this is now left to him: to proclaim the spiritful *nihil* as existence and himself as the new man. Stavrogin is not yet so 'advanced'. All he can do is to kill himself; after all, the 'demonic' game with ideas, crimes, and confessions—this game that has a goal—has proved itself powerless. The decisive moment, excised in the usual version of the novel as abridged by the author, is precisely the failure of the confession: Stavrogin has wanted the holy man to believe in its existential character and thereby help him, Stavrogin, to existence. But existential confession is possible only as a breaking-through to the great action of the high conscience in self-illumination, persevering self-identification, and a reconciling relationship to the world. This possibility, however, is in Stavrogin's eyes one of two things: either essentially not accorded to him or destroyed by him through his life-game. In Dostoevski's own eyes, however, man is redeemable when he wills redemption *as such* and thereby also his share in it—the great act of the high conscience.

6

The Possessed was written in 1870, Kafka's *Trial* in 1915. The
two books represent two basically different but closely connected
situations of human history from which their authors suffered:
the one the uncanny negative certainty, 'Human values are
beginning to shatter', and the other the still more uncanny
uncertainty, 'Do world-meaning and world-order still have any
connection at all with this nonsense and this disorder of the
human world?'—an uncertainty that appears to have arisen out
of that negative certainty.

Everything in Kafka's book is intended to be uncertain and
indefinite, at times to the point of an absurdity, which always
remains artistically mastered. This court of justice before which
Joseph K is unexpectedly cited because of an unnamed and to
him unknown guilt is at once prosaically real and of ghostly
indefiniteness, wild, crude, and senselessly disordered through
and through. But Joseph K is himself, in all his actions, of
hardly less indefiniteness—merely a different kind—as, charged
with guilt, he confusedly carries on day after day a life as
directionless as before. Directionless, that is, except for the
one aim he now pursues, sometimes busily, sometimes incidentally: namely, that of getting free of the court. To this
end he occupies himself with indefinite advocates, indefinite
women, and other indefinite human instruments in order that
they may provide him, in the face of the peculiar ways of this
peculiar court, with the protection that he imagines is all he
needs. The indefinite guilt with which he is charged occupies
him only in so far as he thinks from time to time of composing
a written defence in the form of a short description of his life
which will explain, in connection with each more important
event, on what grounds he then acted thus and not otherwise,
and whether he now approves or condemns his manner of acting
at that time. Finally there happens what is reported in an
unfinished chapter: 'From then on K forgot the court.'

All this is not to be called chaotic, for in a chaos is hidden a
world that shall emerge out of it; here there is no trace of a
cosmos that wills to come into being. But one may well call all
this taken together—the court, the accused, and the people

around him—labyrinthine. The disorder, mounting to absurdity, points toward a secret order, one, however, which nowhere shows itself except by way of a hint, which apparently would first become manifest only if Joseph K did what until the end he does not do—make 'the confession' that is demanded of him. But he cannot, as he says, discover the least guilt on account of which one could accuse him. Indeed, he ends later—clearly without quite knowing what he is saying—by uttering the presumptuous words that are not proper to any human mouth: 'I am completely guiltless.' The thread that leads out of the labyrinth is not to be found in the book; rather this thread exists only when just that happens which did not happen, the 'confession of guilt'.

But what can be meant here, under the given presuppositions, by making a confession? This question hovers in a strange, altogether intentional paradox. A well-informed young woman says to Joseph K, leaning on his shoulder, 'One cannot, in fact, defend oneself against this court; one must make the confession. Make it therefore at the first opportunity. Only then is there any possibility of escaping.' And he answers, 'You understand much about this court and about the deceit that is necessary here'. Since Kafka himself says nothing like this, it can only mean that Joseph, who holds himself, in fact, to be 'entirely guiltless', understands that he should make a false confession, and at this moment he does not seem disinclined to do so. Later, however, a painter, who is likewise, as we hear, well-acquainted with the ways of this court, advises him thus: 'Since you are guiltless, it is really possible for you to rely on your innocence.' Note well: In the same speech the same speaker declares that he has never yet witnessed a single acquittal, but immediately afterwards he says that the decisions of the court were not published, that there exist, however, 'legends' of actual acquittals, and that these legends probably contain 'a certain truth'.

In this atmosphere the action moves forward, and it clearly seems as though the accusation and with it the encouragement to confession are a senseless absurdity, as Joseph K has declared them to be in his speech before the court: 'And the meaning of this great organization, gentlemen? It consists in the fact that innocent persons are arrested, and against them a senseless and for the most part, as in my case, inconsequential proceedings are instituted.' Some Kafka interpreters take these words to express the essential message of the book. This position is refuted through the further course of the action and through notes in Kafka's diaries relating to it.

I have in mind the chapter, 'In the Cathedral', in which is told how Joseph K comes by accident into a church and is here addressed by name by a clergyman unknown to him, the prison chaplain, who also belongs to the organization of the court, but does not act by order of the court. This chapter corresponds exactly to the one excised by Dostoevski from *The Possessed*, in which Stavrogin hands over his confession to the high priest (a chapter which Kafka, moreover, could have known only in an incomplete version, not including the text of the confession). In both a priest is the antagonist, in both it is a matter of a confession of guilt; however, in Dostoevski it is furnished undemanded while in Kafka it is demanded. For it is this demand that the chaplain wishes to convey by the information that the case is going badly, since the court holds the guilt to be proved. 'But I am not guilty,' answers K, 'it's a misunderstanding. And, if it comes to that, how can any man be called guilty? We are all simply men here, one as much as the other.' One must listen closely: What is denied here is the ontic character of guilt, the depth of existential guilt beyond all mere violations of taboos. It is just this that Freud wished to deny when he undertook the relativize guilt feeling genetically. And to Joseph K's reply the priest answers, 'That is true', which means: Indeed we are all men, and should not overestimate the difference between men. He continues, however, 'But that's how all guilty men talk', which means: He who is in question gets off by talking about the others, instead of occupying himself with himself.

Now the priest asks, 'What is the next step you propose to take in the matter?' 'I'm going to seek more help', answers K. 'You cast about too much for outside help', he now hears. And when he still will not understand, the chaplain shrieks at him, 'Can't you see two steps in front of you?' He speaks like one who sees a man, still standing there before him, as already fallen. What he wants to say with his words, without directly saying it, is that the verdict, 'into which the proceedings gradually pass over', now stands at hand, and the verdict itself already means death.

And now, as the last and most extreme effort, the chaplain tells the man, for whose soul and destiny he wrestles in one, the parable of the doorkeeper who stands, as one of countless men, 'before the Law', before one of the countless doors leading into the interior of the Law, and of the man who desires entrance here. This man is frightened by the difficulties that await him who dares entrance, according to the information imparted to him by the doorkeeper. He now passes days and years, the entire remainder of his life, sitting sideways before this one out of innumerably many doors, until shortly before his end the keeper discloses to him that this doorway was destined for him alone and now is going to be shut. Joseph K listens to the parable and does not understand it: What then could the man have done to manage to get in? The clergyman does not tell him. Kafka himself, as he records in his diaries, first understood the significance of the story when he read it aloud to his fiancée. On another occasion, he clearly expressed this significance himself in an unforgettable passage in his notebooks: 'Confession of guilt, unconditional confession of guilt, door springing open, it appears in the interior of the house of the world whose turbid reflection lay behind walls.' The confession is the door springing open. It is the true 'breakthrough', by which word Joseph K is falsely accustomed to describe the aspired-for escape from the law.

What does the legal concept of confession of guilt become here? What is so named here is self-illumination, the first and opening event in the action of the great conscience.

Stavrogin makes a confession in words. He describes therein in horrible detail the course of his crime, but both in remembering it and in recording it he remains incapable of self-illumination. He lacks the small light of humility that alone can illuminate the abyss of the guilty self in broad waves. He seeks for some kind of foothold, no matter how meagre; then he gives up and kills himself.

Joseph K makes no confession; he refuses to understand that

it is necessary for him to do so. In distinction from Stavrogin he is not proud; unlike the latter, he does not distinguish himself from other men. But by that very fact, with his, 'We are all simply men here', he escapes the demand to bear into his inner darkness (of which Kafka speaks in his diaries) the cruel and salutary light. He insists that there is no such thing as personal existential guilt. His innermost being knows otherwise—because Kafka, who is closely connected with Joseph K, knows otherwise—but he shuns penetrating to this innermost being until it is too late. At this point Franz Kafka and Joseph K seem to have to part company. Kafka had imparted to him something of his own name, he had given him to bear (as he gave to 'K' in *The Castle*) his own suffering from a senselessly acting environment; with humorous caricature he had endowed him with his own traits. But now in the decisive hour, according to the logic of the fiction, he lets him say, 'How can any man be called guilty?' and lets him lengthily and ingeniously dispute over the story of the doorkeeper, Kafka's most concentrated statement of his life-view, instead of accepting its teaching. As a result, Kafka, who understands the depth of existential guilt, must separate himself at this point from Joseph K.

He attains connection with him again, however, through the fact that soon afterwards, when the executioners are already leading Joseph K to his death, Kafka lets him concentrate himself in a strong, although still rational, self-recollection. He lets Joseph, who now knows that and how the trial is going to end, say to himself, 'I always wanted to snatch at the world with twenty hands, and not for a very laudable motive, either'. Joseph K has recognized that he has projected on the disordered human world only his own disorder. His self-recollection is not, of course, the beginning of a self-illumination, but it is a first step toward it, without the man who does it knowing it. And now, before the end, Kafka may again take the foolish man to his heart, although at the very end, before the knife falls on Joseph K, Kafka lets the old foolish notions of some still forgotten objections come into his mind. Perhaps Kafka meant himself by the man whom Joseph K glimpses at the last standing in a window, 'a man faint and insubstantial at that distance and at that height': he wants to help his creature and may not.

It might still be asked how the absurd confusion that rules in the court is to be reconciled with the justice of the accusation and the demand. The question places before us a central problem of Kafka's that we find in the background of this novel and of the related novel *The Castle*, where an inaccessible power governs by means of a slovenly bureaucracy. We can extract the answer from an important note in Kafka's diary, from the time of the genesis of *The Trial*, in which he speaks of being occupied with the biblical figure of the unjust judges. It reads, 'I find, therefore, my opinion, or at least the opinion that I have formerly found in me'. Psalm 82, of which he is clearly speaking here, has as its subject God's judgment over those 'sons of God', or angels, to whom He had entrusted the regimen over the human world and who had vilely misused their office and 'judged falsely'. The content of this late psalm is connected with that of the oriental myth, elaborated by the Gnostics, of the astral spirits who fatefully determine the destiny of the world, but from whose power that man may become free who dedicates himself to the concealed highest light and enters into rebirth. I have reason to assume that Kafka also knew this myth at that time.[1] In *The Trial* he modified it, in accord with his own contemplation of the world, through letting the just accusation of an inaccessible highest judgment be conveyed by a disorderly and cruel court. Only that man can escape the arm of this court who, out of his own knowledge, fulfils the demand for confession of guilt according to its truth through executing the primal confession, the self-illumination. Only he enters the interior of the Law.

7

The destiny of both men, that of Stavrogin and that of Joseph K, is determined by their false relationship to their guiltiness.

Stavrogin, of course, plays with the thought of bearing before him like a banner the confession of his most shameful guilt, but he does not bring forth the greater courage to understand in self-illumination his essential being and the origin of his guilt. His feeling, as he says in his last letter, is 'too weak and

[1] I refer to a question concerning this myth that Kafka put to me at the time of his visit to my house in Berlin in 1911 or 1912.

too shallow', his wish 'too little strong; it cannot lead me'. He declares himself unable to kill himself, for 'vexation and shame can never exist in me, and consequently no despair'. But immediately thereafter despair overwhelms him and he gives himself up to death.

Joseph K belongs to another, essentially later, more 'advanced' generation. Not merely before the world, but also before himself, he refuses to concern himself with an ostensible state of guilt. He refuses to find and illuminate in himself the cause of this indictment which this questionable society casts on him from somewhere—say, from an invisible, unknowable 'highest court'. Indeed, it now passes as proved, in this his generation, that no real guilt exists; only guilt feeling and guilt convention. Until the last moment he refuses to enter through the door that still stands open and is only apparently shut; thus the verdict overtakes him.

Both Stavrogin and Joseph K have not taken the crucial hour of man upon themselves, and now have lost it.

It is the crucial hour of man of which we speak. For, to use Pascal's language, the greatness of man is bound up with his misery.

Man is the being who is capable of becoming guilty and is capable of illuminating his guilt.

I have illustrated through two examples from epic literature the manifold resistance of the human being against self-illumination. But this inner resistance is entirely different from the patient's struggle, well known to the psychoanalyst, against his efforts to convey from the unconscious into the conscious[1] a repressed state of facts of a guiltlike nature. For the guilt which is in question here is not at all repressed into the unconscious. The bearer of existential guilt remains in the realm of conscious existence. This guilt is not one that allows itself to be repressed into the unconscious. It remains in the chamber of memory, out of which it can at any moment penetrate unexpectedly into that of consciousness, without it being possible for any barriers to be erected against this invasion. The memory receives all experiences and actions without the

[1] Freud, *A General Introduction to Psychoanalysis* (New York: Liveright, 1920), see Lecture 19.

assistance of man. It may, however, retain the ingredients of what is remembered in such a manner that what ascends into the actual remembering does not enter it in its original character. The existential guilt, therefore, does not enter it as such. Only when the human person himself overcomes his inner resistance can he attain to self-illumination.

The 'opening door' of self-illumination leads us into no place beyond the law, but into the interior of the law. It is the law of man in which we then stand: the law of the identity of the human person as such with himself, the one who recognizes guilt with the one who bears guilt, the one in light with the one in darkness. The hard trial of self-illumination is followed by the still harder, because never ceasing, trial of persevering in this self-identification. But by this is not meant an ever renewed scourging of the soul with its knowledge of its abyss understood as something inevitably allotted to it. What is meant is an upright and calm perseverance in the clarity of the great light.

If a man were only guilty toward himself, in order to satisfy the demanding summons that meets him at the height of conscience, he would only need to take this one road from the gate of self-illumination, that of persevering. But a man is always guilty toward other beings as well, toward the world, toward the being that exists over against him. From self-illumination he must, in order to do justice to the summons, take not one road but two roads, of which the second is that of reconciliation. By reconciliation is understood here that action from the height of conscience that corresponds on the plane of the law to the customary act of reparation. In the realm of existential guilt one cannot, of course, 'make reparation' in the strict sense—as if the guilt with its consequences could thereby be recalled, as it were. Reconciliation means here, first of all, that I approach the man toward whom I am guilty in the light of my self-illumination (in so far as I can still reach him on earth) acknowledge to his face my existential guilt and help him, in so far as possible, to overcome the consequences of my guilty action. But such a deed can be valid here only as reconciliation if it is done not out of a premeditated resolution, but in the unarbitrary working of the existence I have achieved. And this can happen, naturally, only out of the core of a transformed relationship to the world, a new service to the world with the renewed forces of the renewed man.

This is not the place to speak of the events in the sphere of faith that correspond to the events in the sphere of the high conscience that we have just discussed. For the sincere man of faith, the two spheres are so referred to each other in the practice of his life, and most especially when he has gone through existential guilt, that he cannot entrust himself exclusively to either of them. Both, the human faith not less than the human conscience, can err and err again. And knowing about this their erring, both—conscience not less than faith—must place themselves in the hands of grace. It is not for me to speak in general terms of the inner reality of him who refuses to believe in a transcendent being with whom he can communicate. I have only this to report: that I have met many men in the course of my life who have told me how, acting from the high conscience as men who had become guilty, they experienced themselves as seized by a higher power. These men grew into an existential state to which the name of rebirth is due.

8

With all this, I repeat, the psychotherapist in his medical intercourse with his patients has nothing directly to do, not even when he ventures in a particular case to set for himself the goal of an existential healing. The utmost that can be expected of him, as I have said, is only this: that, reaching out beyond his familiar methods, he conduct the patient, whose existential guilt he has recognized, to where an existential help of the self can begin. But to do this, he must know about the reality toward which I have tried to point in this chapter.

CHAPTER VII

MAN AND HIS IMAGE-WORK[1]

———————

1

The question of the connection between the essence of man and the essence of art must be posed anew. That means that art must be regarded as the image-work of man, the peculiar image-work of his peculiarity. We ask about the connection between what is essentially peculiar to man and what is essentially characteristic of art.

At the beginning of a part of asking and of seeking an answer must always stand the clarification of the question from which one proceeds, preventing all confusion by making sure of its unambiguity. It must consequently become clear that our question may not be confused either with the historical-prehistorical question about the origin of art in the evolution of the human race or with the psychological question about its origin in the inner life of the artist. These two questions, incidentally, treat the essentially hidden—that which is hidden in the 'that time' of the primeval or in the 'there' of the creative person—as something essentially given instead of approaching it with rigorous self-restraint, cautiously interpreting the given works. We do not ask: How did art once arise? nor even: How does it arise ever again in each genuine work anew? but rather: What can be said about art as about a being that springs from the being of man?

Our question is an anthropological one in the philosophical sense of the word. In saying this, it must be borne in mind, of course, that every anthropology of a subject touches on its

[1] Trans. by Maurice Friedman.

139

ontology, hence that every investigation of a subject in its conditioning by the manner, the nature, the attitude of man leads us toward this subject's place in being and its function in meaning. For according as we fathom the relation of a circuit of reality to us, we are always referred to its still unfathomed relation to being and meaning!

Now, however, after the possible confusion and blurring of outlines of the question have been eliminated, a problem discloses itself at its heart. We ask about art, but does art exist in sufficient concreteness to accredit the question about it? Is it not merely the arts that exist in such concreteness? What we ask about is the artistic, the common principle that we find effectively present in sufficient concreteness in each of the arts. When Johann Georg Hamann[1] stirred up the revolt of living speech against routine and thus finally only worked together with the revolt raised soon after by his antagonist Immanuel Kant—that of unbiased formation of concepts against rationalist convention—the designation of the creative arose. To our time, which is 'indigent' indeed but devoted to a commendable sobriety, this all too pathetic metaphor has begun to be repugnant. For our concern, however, the original biblical category is above all unusable because it places too great a demand on the specifically human, about which it is concerned. Today we are obliged to proceed more exactly here. Creation means originally and decisively a bringing forth, certainly not out of nothing but out of the creating itself; it is independent of all otherness, but we may only hope for an anthropological understanding of art if we take account of the dependence of man on that which exists independently of him.

The path of our question must begin in the sphere in which the life of the human senses dwells; it is that in which the dependence of man on the existent properly constitutes itself and that which determines the reality-character of all art so that no

---

[1] Johann Georg Hamann, 1730–88. German pietist philosopher who was radically opposed both to the rationalism of the Enlightenment and to the systematic idealism of Kant. He opposed Kant by emphasizing the productive power of experience, intuition, and feeling. He saw nature and revelation as the true sources of all knowledge, reason as secondary to faith in relation to cognition and action. See Ronald Gregor Smith, *J. G. Hamann, Study in Christian Existence with Selections from His Writing* (New York: Harper & Row; London: Collins 1960). Ed.

mental and no emotional element may enter into art otherwise than through becoming a thing of the senses. Another path could be taken only by a radical idealism that would understand all notion of the senses as product of the sovereign subject. We can no longer do this, we who are unavoidably set before a world that is, certainly, again and again immanent in our souls but is not originally immanent in it, a world which manifests itself as transcending the soul precisely in the course of that becoming immanent in it which is happening at any given time. The artist is not a slave to nature, but free as he may hold himself of it and far as he may remove himself from it, he may establish his work only by means of what happens to him in the sphere of the bound life of his senses—in the fundamental events of perception, which is a meeting with the world and ever again a meeting with the world.

2

It is worth noting that Conrad Fiedler,[1] the aesthetician of the imaging arts who, so far as I know, was the first to pose the question of the origin of art out of the constitution of man, was an adherent of post-Kantian idealism. Standing in the transition between two ages, he anticipated our anthropological question, but without its true content, which is the meeting. The transitional character of his thought is clearly expressed in a decisive word of his formulation of the question. 'The question about the origin of art out of the constitution of the spiritual nature of man', he writes, 'is the first and most important one which can be posed in the realm of philosophical observations of art.' The word in this sentence that I call decisive is the attribute 'spiritual'. We no longer limit the question thus. What is specifically human, what decisively sets man apart from all other living beings and provides the factual basis for our discussion cannot be grasped by the concept of spirituality. The whole body-soul person is the human in man; it is this wholeness which is involved in his meeting with the world. From this it follows that the question that we ask is concerned with it. We

[1] Conrad Fiedler, 1814–75, the German aesthetician who foresaw the trends of modern architecture by stressing 'functionalism'. Ed.

no longer begin from above, and certainly not from below, but from everywhere.

Fiedler, nearly ninety years ago, came astonishingly near to the insight of our days; he was prevented from taking the next step by his imprisonment in idealism. 'The capacity for knowledge', so reads his most pregnant thesis, 'contains a law-giving that makes necessary the artistic formation of the sense perceptions.' This thesis is correct in seeing the formation as going beyond the perception, incorrect in seeing this as deter-mined by the capacity for knowledge. Fiedler regards 'the knowing penetration' as a kind of formation which is supple-mented by the artistic. But one misses the basic nature of art through which it becomes corporeal if one moves it so close to knowledge, indeed directly subsumes it under the latter. Thinking and art certainly supplement each other, but not like two connected organs; rather they are like the electric poles between which the spark jumps.

Fiedler rightly sees in the artistic activity a 'natural further development' of the event of perception; but he injures his insight by tying it to the doctrine of the world-producing subject. As a corrective to it, we must go back to that saying of Albrecht Dürer's, often cited but seldom basically thought through, which was also a standard for Fiedler: 'For art truly is hidden in nature; he who can tear it out, has it.' We are obliged to interpret with care this remarkable expression of a great experience.

A thinker of our own time, Martin Heidegger, has included an interpretation of this saying of Dürer's among the analyses of concepts of which his essay on the origin of the work of art is composed, masterly executed operations but ones which attack language and its spokenness with all too rough, all too intention-laden a hand. '*Reissen*' (to tear), thus it is there inter-preted, 'heisst hier Herausholen des Risses und den Riss reissen mit der Reissfeder auf dem Reissbrett' (*Reissen* in the sense of 'tearing' is identified here with *reissen* as 'drawing'· done on the 'drawing board'), and to this he adds sketch (*Aufriss*) and design (*Grundriss*), but also strife as split (*Riss*) is implied. Dürer's simple profundity[1] is swallowed up by this

[1] The competent contemporary of Dürer's, Camerarius, translates it: *Quam si extrahere potueris.*

wholly different profundity of word-associative combinations and complications.

To the simple reader to whom Dürer speaks, and I dare to confirm his simple understanding in opposition to so grandiose a deed of violence, it says to him that what is imprisoned in another substance at times cannot be gently drawn from it but must be 'torn' out of it by force, and such an action Albrecht Dürer believes the composed force of the strong artist capable of. The reader whom he really addressed, the young painter, shall feel: 'So deep as it is thus hidden, so resistant as it is delivered up, so strong and well must I work.' He can still feel it today. And we reflecting laymen of today also still let Dürer speak to us—not in order to illuminate our own trains of thought by the prismatic fullness of association of his lucid formulation, but in order to communicate with Dürer himself and to experience with understanding how and in how far we may receive his word.

What Dürer here means by art and immediately after explains as 'learned art which is propagated by seed, grows up and brings fruit of its kind', that is the knowledge, handed down from the teaching to the learning artist, about that intercourse with nature which draws forth. Only through it and out of it is 'the collected hidden treasure of the heart' legitimately and without arbitrariness 'revealed through the work and the new creature'. This concept of art we can today honestly and faithfully receive only if it first proves to be the case that it holds not only for what Dürer called nature, but also for what we call nature.

In his interpretation, Heidegger treats the word 'nature' as needing no discussion. In my opinion, we may not proceed thus. We must now ask what the word 'nature' means to us men of today, to us the amazed witnesses holding out against modern nuclear physics. Wherein does it have its reality for us?

3

What Dürer calls nature is simply the world of the senses thought of as existing independently of us.

Our life in the world is bound to an insuperable divergence.

143

It is the notorious discrepancy between the penetrating images of our perception, which are to be found, however, only in the sphere of our relation to the existing being and nowhere else, and a physically or at least mathematically comprehensible substratum underlying them, as we are accustomed to say; a substratum, however, that nowhere and never is accessible to us in a reality. We assign these to two or more strictly separate provinces of scientific knowledge and resign ourselves to the idea that a unity of conceptual life in the world is simply unattainable by us. Dürer did not need to concern himself with this divergence. The world of the senses, the clarification of whose phenomena one always sought in investigation and deliberation, was then still uncritically accepted as that in which we live, as just the nature in which we are set and to which we are referred.

This understanding with nature is that which was still three centuries later maintained in the human circle in which the characteristic euphoria before the death of a world-era manifested itself, in Goethe's circle, despite all the enormous investigating and pondering that went on. Its valid expression is that fragment of 1782 that is superscribed 'nature'. It, nature, that which incessantly speaks to us, does not, to be sure, divulge its mystery to us, but it is extolled as trustworthy to the point of 'benevolence'. One already speaks here, to be sure—a while before Hegel's 'world-reason'—of a 'ruse' that she exercises, but also of a 'good goal' of this ruse. 'I confide myself to her'—so speaks here the confession to nature.

We can no longer confide ourselves thus. A nature to which one could confess thus we no longer know. No matter how much we are gripped by that hymnlike expression of a great enthusiasm for an all-unity which is beheld and praised as working, as living, as sensing, indeed, positively as loving— a no less great, an unbreakable resistance is in us against the faith that bears it. The realm of modes of observation into which our relation to the world has disintegrated no longer offers a unity of this kind to whose life our life could relate itself as a unity. The new 'world-image' ultimately consists in the fact that there is no longer an *image* of the world.

And nonetheless, we who are seeking for the anthropological

meaning of art may start from Dürer's saying. It must be made clear why and how we may do so.

The artist, says Dürer, tears art out of nature, in which it is hidden. We cannot hold this saying valid for the world of the senses: it has its being for us now only in the conditionality of the perception which, to be sure, catches what it catches from a world independent of us, but communicates to us only properties that are not to be found in it.

One has rightly called our age the heroic age of physics. I add to this that it is the age of a heroic resignation which is connected with this heroism of physics. It is not really science that is resigned. That a group of phenomena must, say, be explained through two mutually exclusive theories does not trouble it, science. It sees in it perhaps a 'wonderful trick' of nature (Pascual Jordan) or contents itself with attesting—as Niels Bohr has once done—that as the consequence of the new situation in physics even the words 'to be' and 'to know' have lost their simple meaning. It is otherwise with man in so far as he is not a physicist. He still desires, even in the post-Goethean age, to live in a world of which one can form an image—not merely imageable in a symbolic way, but as a real world constituted in a certain way. For to live in an unrepresentable world entails a contradiction which can become hopeless if borne in untransparent immanence. But now the mode of being of the space–time world as a whole and that of each part of it have become unrepresentable, indeed, this mode runs diametrically opposed to everything that can be represented as world, that it, it is no longer capable of being received in lived life as the world of this life.

Our present relation to the world resembles that told in Egyptian myth of the relation to the god whose secret names one has learned, which knowledge one may use like a bundle of powers. The basic mathematical formulae agree, a kind of symbol at once abstract and practical; experiment confirms it, and the technical application confirms it; but now for the first time the uncanny strangeness of the world is perceived. That which I designate and use, that before whose incomprehensibility I shudder is fearfully dual; in place of the powerfully trustworthy to which I confide myself stands the embodied contradiction.

I recall an hour that I spent over forty years ago in conversation with Albert Einstein. I had been pressing him in vain with a concealed question about his faith. Finally he burst forth. 'What we [and by this "we" he meant we physicists] strive for', he cried, 'is just to draw his lines after *Him*.' To draw after—as one retraces a geometrical figure. That already seemed to me then an innocent hubris; since then the questionableness of such strivings has become far more serious still. The fundamental impossibility of investigating the electron, the 'complementarity' of contradictory explanations—and the lines of being that God has drawn! And nonetheless we must proceed from this unimageable, unrealizable, uncanny, unhomelike world if we want to find the nature of which we ourselves may say that art is hidden in it and is to be 'torn' out of it.

4

Our behaviour rests upon innumerable unifications of movements to something and perceptions of something. There is no movement that is not directly or indirectly connected with a perception, and no perception that is not more or less consciously connected with a movement. There is nothing in and of us that is fully removed from this base; even the images of fantasy, dreams, madness draw their material from it; our language is rooted in it, its subtlest ramifications draw from it its sap, and along with language is rooted in it our thought, which cannot renounce it without losing its link with life; mathematics itself must concretize itself ever again in the relationship to it.

That toward which we move and which we perceive is always, understood from the standpoint of my intention, a thing of the senses, and even when I myself am the object of my perceiving movement and moving perception, I must in some measure make use of my corporeality in order so to effect my relationship to myself that I satisfy my intention. It is otherwise when I seek to grasp the object as independent of my movement and perception. If it is I myself that is in question, then to the extent that I now become in such a manner 'I', I simply cease to be object. That holds equally for every other

'I' in genuine communication with me: he is to me only partner, not object; as partner, as my 'Thou' the other can be grasped in his full independence without curtailing his sense nature. But this is not the case with all objects proper or what are treated as objects, to which I can neither ascribe any 'I' or whose 'I' I cannot here and now make present to myself. All this I can only place in its independence by freeing it from the sense world, from its sensible representation. What then remains as it-self, emptied of all the properties that it has acquired in the meeting with me, in the sense world, may here be designated by a small x. It exists but not as imagable. We could, to be sure, attempt to leave it some of the properties that it possessed in the world of the senses, but then we only set it in a fictitious middle sphere that hovers midway between the sensible and the independent. Of x we know what Kant points out to us of the thing in-itself, namely, that it is. Kant would say: 'And nothing more', but we who live today must add: 'And that the existent meets us.' This is, if we take it seriously enough, a powerful knowing. For in all the world of the senses there is no trait that does not stem from meetings, that does not originate in the co-working of the x in the meeting.

An ancient linden tree once stood on the path that I took time after time. I always accepted it as it was given to me, and that was enough for me. Until one time the question seized me: 'Now that I meet the linden it is thus—how is it before, how is it after our meeting? What is it when no perception approaches it?' The philosophical schools of thought commanded me to reject the question as meaningless, but I resisted. Botany answered the question with a reckoning about the structure and dynamics of the linden, but of the properties of the linden that I perceived, I could not preserve anything thereby. For the green of the leaf that fluttered down on my hand chlorophyll had to be substituted, and this, like all that which was said to me of the biochemical findings about the life of the tree, drew me into the world of x where there existed only that which could not be realized. Even the space in which the linden was fixed was unrealizable mathema. But I put up with it, I accepted the thing or unthing, which had become property-less and uncanny, the thing that had waited for me in order to become once again the blooming and fragrant linden of my sense world. I said to the sense-deprived linden-x what Goethe said to the fully sensible rose: 'So it is you.'

As the linden tree waited for me in order to become green, so did nature, the unperceived, x-nature, once wait for living beings to arise through whose meeting perception the green, the soft, the warm—all the qualities conditioned by the senses —should come into the world. But the animal lives, as the biology of our day has recognized (I cite the Dutch physiologist and psychologist Frederick J. J. Buytendijk), 'with his environment as with his organs'; it perceives nothing more and nothing other than what and how the actual situation demands that it perceive. It enters into the functional circle and knows outside of its own needs and dangers hardly anything of other things and beings. Thus nature, because it strives for completion and that means also for being perceived, looked for one who would make possible its new constitution, to allow the existent to appear at a distance, as something existing beyond his needs and wishes, to detach and remove it from himself. It is only through him that it has become nature in the real sense of the term, as a whole that may enter part after part into manifestation. Man belongs in nature not merely with his vital acts, not merely as one who moves, but also as one who perceives. My perception is, without prejudice to all spiritually arising from my being a subject, a natural act in which 'I' and x take part.

Let us proceed confidently from x, from its unfathomable darkness: its being has intercourse with my being when it dispatches to my senses the representatives to which scientific language has lent the ambiguous name of stimuli, and out of our intercourse arise the clearly outlined forms that people my sense world in colour and sound. It itself, the sense world, arises out of the intercourse of being with being.

Which connections correspond in the ontic of x to the forms of this our world? We know nothing about it. But when we gaze into the life-depths of our perception, we learn that here as everywhere forming is not a making. From each unrealizable connection in the x-world there shoots upward to us a multiplicity, just those so-called stimuli; it is as if it disintegrated into these stimuli in order to reach us. But here each multi-plicity enters into a formed unity, my senses work together with it in close association—and the particular linden stands before me. Indeed, even the rustling and fragrance is not merely in and on it; it itself rustles and smells, and it is it itself that I feel when my hand touches its bark. From the wholly un-sensible connection in x that meets me the wholly sensible correspondence has arisen that now stands in its place as a being in nature, with its existence dependent on me and those like me.

Even when I wander in the desert and nowhere a form offers itself to my eye, even when a crude noise strikes my ear, there takes place in my perception binding and limiting, joining and rhythmizing, the becoming of a formed unity. The truer, the more existentially reliably it takes place, so much the more, in all realms of sense, is observation transformed into vision. Vision is figurating[1] faithfulness to the unknown and does its work in co-operation with it. It is faithfulness not to the appear-ance, but to being—to the inaccessible with which we associate.

5

In human perception, so we may say, something which was hidden in nature is drawn and lifted out of it. It is not, to be sure, art. But one may label it 'visibility' (in the pregnant sense of that which can be apprehended in vision). All visibility, the visibility of all the senses, has a direction toward figuration. If there is also in x something like the chaotic, which I do not hold to be impossible, then nothing of it enters into the visibility.

All perception, but especially that deepened to vision, is intent on figure. Figurating, it gives the unsensible connections of the x-world the entirely present correspondence. Only the artist, however, is 'full of figure'. Only his vision which is a working vision adds to the first world formation, achieved by man as such, the second full figuration which is, of course, in still far higher measure than the first a personal one, and thus immeasurably manifold. All perception of all human genera-

[1] In the sense of making the figure fully manifest. M.B.

tions is, as figuration, preliminary. The sense world is only a stage.

The world filter in the structure of human senses, of course, yields far more than that of any other living beings known to us, but it is not constituted differently: It shall deliver what the species *Homo sapiens* needs in order to exist, and that is, of course, a whole mass, but technically limited. Man is not yet as a species adapted to figurating in the vision. Persons reach personal attainment in the limits of filter construction. But there is something that goes beyond that, that begins at any given time where the function of the filter is at an end, a bodily element that sends itself out, as it were—in order to partake of a ground that otherwise would not be grasped—in enormous variety of manners and persons, nonetheless producing a unity of unities and with each new work renewing it. I mean the existence of the artist; I mean art. Perception draws out of the being the world that we need; only vision and, in its wake, art transcends need and makes the superfluous into the necessary.

The artist is the man who instead of objectifying what is over against him forms it into an image. Here the nature of the action in which perception takes place no longer suffices: the working must play a substantial part if that which stands over against him is to become image. That which stands over against, I say; that does not mean this or that phenomenon, this or that piece of the external world, some complex of appearance given to the sight or hearing in the actual experience, but whatever in the whole possible world-sphere enters into that sense with which this particular art is associated, the whole possible world-sphere of sight, the whole possible world-sphere of hearing. This and nothing less than this is that by which the artist exercises what Jean Paul—in distinction from the power of imagination, 'which animals also have since they dream and they fear'—calls the power of formation, that which 'makes all parts into a whole' and establishes the freedom 'whereby the beings move in their ether like suns'.

Dürer thinks of the artist as standing over against the world of the senses, but this world of the senses ever again comes into being only in standing over against, if also, so to speak, with the assistance of all past generations that have elaborated our seeing-relation and our hearing-relation into a world. The artistic standing over against, however, itself happens between the being of the artist—not his perception alone, but his being —and the being of the x. In so far as he is an artist, he perceives it artistically, that is, by virtue of the completed figuration, the becoming of the image.

A poet of our time, Paul Valéry, has come close to the truth suitable to us, but only in order at the same instant to remove himself from it. He sees the world order 'which the demiurgos has lifted out of the confusion of the beginning', as given to the architect as chaos and primal matter whereby, in order to satisfy man in particular, he completes the uncompleted work. One notes how wonderfully the true and the false are mingled here. The Doric column is not added to a prefounded world order, but rather is brought forth in the work out of proportions hidden until then. Architecture discovers the relations ever anew—through the work and in it; they must be discovered ever anew. When the young Goethe once undertook to clear up for himself what it is that he called the creative power in the artist he wrote, 'surging feeling of relations, measures and what is necessary to them'. What is reported to us of Beethoven's walks, 'how, notebook and pencil in hand, he often stood standing as if listening, looked up and down and then jotted down notes on the paper', is for us an almost mythical image of just this actuality. Artistic fantasy is in its innermost being discovery through figuration.

The experiences of artistic standing over against the world and the conditions of the figurations unite for the artist into the sphere of being decisive for his art—for the plastic arts an optical, for music an acoustical sphere of being. With *one* exception each of these spheres is determined by a single sense; experiences of the other senses cannot gain a footing in it, they can only be related to it. Every artistic activity is made possible through an elemental renunciation, through a productive shrinking of the world to the exclusiveness of a single sphere. In it the artist lives, in so far as he lives as artist; in it he rules figurating, in the greatness of such loss and gain. Only *one* art has a sphere that is not sufficiently determined by one of the senses, but rather itself lives above the level of the senses; it is poetry. Poetry does not originate from one of the senses' standing over against the world, but from the primal structure of man as man, his primal structure founded upon sense experiences and overarched by the spirit's power of symbols, from language. Even when one tries to grasp the determination of the spheres objectively and instead of sight and hearing speaks of space and time, language remains for poetry as a third. The other arts create out of the spheres of space and time; they are obliged to them and do justice to them: painting by preserving the interrelations of things while renouncing their corporeality; the plastic arts by erecting in this space the corporeal individual being while renouncing its interrelations; architecture by transforming in this space the proportions, the functional relations, the geometric structures in the midst of the unmathematical reality which it thereby also hides; music by embodying time itself in tones, as though, indeed, there were no space. But poetry is not obedient to anything other than language, whether it calls and praises, narrates, or allows the happening between men to unfold in dialogue.

6

One may ask from where the urge to figuration and with it the growth of aptitude for it stems. Why has the species man not contented itself with allowing the formed world of the senses to proceed out of its meetings with x? Why this superimposing of a superformation of the form? Above the x-world and the sense world this third? Why has the species sent forth from itself this special being that removes himself from the norms, the 'artist'? How has the superfluous succeeded to such powers?

To answer these questions we must again proceed, first of all, from the situation of meeting. Over against the x that meets him man is, to begin with, referred to his senses, which make the primally alien his own as something familiar. But he reaches beyond what they give him, he expects more from them, the deepening into the figurative vision, for the sake of the figuration in the work. He exceeds the needed for the sake of the intended. What does that mean?

To go further in seeking an answer here we must ascertain

at the same time the anthropological place of art among the four potencies with which man transcends the natural and establishes the human as a unique realm of being.

In the course of becoming human there appear, incomprehensible in their origin, two constituent factors of the human person closely bound to each other: dissatisfaction with being limited to needs and longing for perfected relation.

Going beyond the satisfaction of needs is common to man and animal. The expression of this common trait is play. But with man as man a new, unheard of thing sets in beyond this. That which answers the purposes of the human species, the firm total structure of using and getting and, surrounding it, the ruffle of relaxing, loosening play, again and again fails to satisfy the human person. With the awakening of personhood awakes the dissatisfaction with the whole natural receiving of what is allotted and with it the 'free' extra allowance that *Homo ludens* treats himself to. But at the same time there arises in the person, binding itself in the most remarkable way with this dissatisfaction, that which I call the longing for perfected relation or for perfection in the relation. The imperfect relations belong to the world of needing and getting or to its play-annexes. But the human person desires more than this. He does not content himself with the measure and degree of the development of relations that are required for the mastering of the needs of daily life and for entering into the regulated freedoms of play: the higher wish appears. In it the genuineness of the person becomes manifest.

Here is disclosed to us the vestibule out of which open the doors of the four potencies in the inner rooms of knowledge, love, art, and faith. They all stand against the world becoming alien, assist us against its alienation.

The man who has become a person knows, like every man, objects of all sorts. All human knowing is relation to an object. The pre-personal individual is satisfied with the knowledge that enables him to deal with the present and perhaps the next hour of existence by means, so to speak, of a life-technical unification with the object. The man who has become a person simply is not satisfied with that. He wants through his knowing of the object 'to get to the bottom'. He makes it his object ever again to attain the perfection of the knowledge relation. This he can do, of course, only through the fact that in investigating one object he excludes all others in so far as they are not necessary for the clarification of this one. Perfected knowledge relation means exclusive knowing that now, of course, attains its height in receiving all that pertains to it in hospitable responsibility.

The other potency is love. The sphere of using and getting, it goes without saying, is here not merely to be understood psychophysically, in the sex act and the movements playing around it, but also sociologically, in the continuity of marriage and family; so far, indeed, the animal and man reach a common province. But the essential love of two beings that is added to that province, that which penetrates both the contact of the sexes and the founding of the generations and transforms them into fully human existence, stems out of another realm in which the dissatisfaction with the world of using and getting and the longing for the perfection of relation blend. And again exclusiveness comes into its own. In all love to man—I mean, naturally, not the performance of duty that takes place in so-called neighbour love, but the earnest affirmation of the human person as such—there shines forth perfected relation.

All this dissatisfaction and longing, exclusiveness and inclusiveness, we find again in the realm of art. The artist, whose meetings with x are of an intensity peculiar to him, does not content himself with beholding what the common human world of the senses makes perceptible to him. He wants, in that sphere among the senses to which his art is oriented, to experience and realize the perfection of the relation to the substratum of the sense things: through the figuration in the vision and in work. He does not portray the form, he does not really remould it; he drives it—not just in the individual object, but in the whole fullness of possibility of this one sense, in so far as it opens itself to him; he drives it into its perfection in its fully figured reality, and the whole optical, the whole acoustical field becomes refashioned ever anew. And already the power of exclusiveness has become apparent to us: the working of all other senses must be cut in order that the working of this one may attain to such perfection in the imprint of its art. But the life of all the other senses is secretly included in the working and the work; deep correspondences, magical evocations exist here, and our concrete understanding is enriched when we succeed, say, in becoming aware of the rhythm in a work of sculpture.

In this context I can only refer to the last potency, the highest, which comprehends and overlaps all the others—faith. How dissatisfaction and longing, exclusiveness and inclusiveness are transformed here is clear to everyone who has been permitted to enter this sphere.

It cannot be in question for us to investigate the prehistorical or ethnologically comprehensible pre-times or pre-stages of knowledge or love or art or religion. We cannot simply disregard them, however. In so far as they are at all accessible to us in their motivations, they appear still to belong wholly to the world of using and getting; a pre-form of the dissatisfaction and longing of which we speak may, nonetheless, be discovered in many of these motivations. When, as the ethnologists report to us, in an exogamous tribe a boy, despite the inexorable laws of the tribe, woos a maiden of his own clan and perseveres in his rebellion to the finally unavoidable suicide, then this individual action cannot be explained by the norms of using and getting. And if in paleolithic times another boy paints on the ceiling of his cave a brown-red bison whose concentration has not been surpassed by any painting of the following ten thousand years, then almost nothing speaks, to be sure, against an explanation of the painting as magic of the hunt. Yet behind this cannot there be felt a dim preconscious desire to get at the hidden kernel of the animal phenomenon through an overfiguration of his visibility?

It is, indeed, neither the mystery of the things nor that of the spirit that is represented in art, but the relation between the two. If I may quote myself: 'Art . . . is the work and witness of the relation between the *substantia humana* and the *substantia rerum*, it is the realm of "the between" which has become a form' (p. 66). Therefore, it is also permissible for us to say that it is given to man as a peculiar special nature to tear art out of nature in which it is hidden. The artist does this not through trying to penetrate behind the world of the senses, but through perfecting its form to the completed image. In the completion, however, we find the origin.

155

APPENDIX

Dialogue between Martin Buber and Carl R. Rogers

EDITOR'S NOTE: *On April 18, 1957, I moderated a dialogue between Martin Buber and the American psychologist Carl R. Rogers as part of a Midwest Conference on Martin Buber organized by the University of Michigan. Beyond the explicit references that Carl R. Rogers had made in his writings to Martin Buber's I–Thou relationship, I was so struck by the resemblances between the two thinkers that, on the basis of then unpublished papers which Dr Rogers sent me, I devoted three pages of the 'Psychotherapy' chapter of my* Martin Buber: The Life of Dialogue *to a comparison of the attitudes of the two toward psychology. Since then I have also become aware of important differences in their approach, and it was in particular this dialogue between them that brought out these differences, even while comfirming their affinity in many basic respects. I have suggested to Martin Buber that this dialogue be included as an Appendix to his anthropology because it makes clear some points that are only implicit in his writings while elaborating on the significance of his anthropology for psychotherapy that is already touched on in a number of his essays in* The Knowledge of Man. *I have made some very minor editorial changes and deletions to facilitate the readability of the dialogue, but I have changed nothing of substance.*

MAURICE FRIEDMAN: I think this is a most significant meeting, not just in terms of psychotherapy, but of the fact that both Martin Buber and Carl Rogers have won our admiration as persons with an approach to personal relations and personal becoming. There are so many remarkable similarities between their thoughts that it is intriguing to have the privilege of hearing them talk with one another and also of seeing what issues may come out. My role as moderator is only, if the occasion should arise, to sharpen these issues or to interpret one way or another. Dr Rogers has been famous for a great many years as the founder of the once so-called nondirective therapy, now re-christened client-centred therapy, and is the Director of the University of Chicago Counseling Center,[1] where he has had very fruitful relations with the theological faculty and the Personality and Religion courses. Doctor Rogers will raise questions with Doctor Buber and Doctor Buber will respond.

[1] Dr Carl R. Rogers is now Professor of Psychology and Psychiatry, the University of Wisconsin. Ed.

156

CARL R. ROGERS: One thing I would say before starting to talk with Doctor Buber is that this is most certainly an unrehearsed dialogue. It was only an hour or two ago that I met Doctor Buber, even though I had met him a long time ago in his writing.

I think that the first question I would like to ask you, Doctor Buber, may sound a trifle impertinent, but I would like to explain it and then perhaps it won't seem impertinent. I have wondered, How have you lived so deeply in interpersonal relationships and gained such an understanding of the human individual, without being a psychotherapist? [Buber laughs.] The reason I ask is that it seems to me that a number of us have come to sense and experience some of the same kinds of learnings that you have expressed in your writing, but very frequently we have come to those learnings through our experience in psychotherapy. I think that there is something about the therapeutic relationship that gives us permission, almost formal permission, to enter into a deep and close relationship with a person, and so we tend to learn very deeply in that way. I think of one psychiatrist friend of mine who says that he never feels as whole, or as much of a person, as he does in his therapeutic interviews. And I share that feeling. And so, if it is not too personal, I would be interested in hearing what were the channels of knowing that enabled you to learn so deeply of people and of relationships?

MARTIN BUBER: That is rather a biographical question. I think I must give instead of one answer, two. One is that I'm not entirely a stranger in, let me say, psychiatry, because when I was a student long ago I studied three terms psychiatry and what they call in Germany *Psychiatrische-Klinique*. I was most interested in the latter. You see, I did not study psychiatry in order to become a psychotherapist. I studied it three terms: first with Flechsig in Leipzig, where there were students of Wundt. Afterwards in Berlin with Mendel, and a third term with Bleuler in Zurich, which was the most interesting of the three. I was then a very young, inexperienced, and not very understanding young man. But I had the feeling that I wanted to know about man, and man in the so-called pathological state. I doubted even then if it is the right term. I wanted to see, if possible to meet, such people and, as far as I can remember, to establish relations, a real relation between what we call a sane man and what we call a pathological man. And this I learned in some measure—as far as a boy of twenty or so can learn such things.

About what mainly constituted what you ask, it was something other. It was just a certain inclination to meet people. And as far as possible, to change something in the *other*, but also to let *me* be changed by *him*. At any event, I had no resistance—put no resistance to it. I began as a young man. I felt I have not the right to want to change another if I am not open to be changed by him as far as it is legitimate. Something is to be changed and his touch, his concept is able to change it more or less. I *cannot* be so to say above him and say, 'No! I'm out of the play. *You* are mad.' There were two phases of it. The first phase went until the year 1918, meaning until I was about forty. And then I, in 1918, I felt something rather strange. I felt that I had been strongly influenced by something that came to an end just then, meaning the First World War. In the course of the war, I did not feel very much about this influence. But at the end I felt, 'Oh, I have been terribly influenced', because I could not resist what went on, and I was compelled to, may I say, to live it. Things that went on just at this moment. You may call this *imagining the real*. Imagining what was going on. This imagining, for four years, influenced me terribly. Just when it was finished, it finished by a certain episode in May 1919 when a friend of mine, a great friend, a great man, was killed by the antirevolutionary soldiers in a very barbaric way,[1] and now again once more—and this was the last time —I was compelled to imagine just this killing, but not in an optical way alone, but may I say so, just with my *body*. And this was the decisive moment, after which, after some days and nights in this state, I felt, 'Oh, something has been done to me'. And from then on, these meetings with people, particularly with young people were— became—in a somewhat different form. I had a decisive experience, experience of four years, many concrete experiences, and from now on, I had to give something more than just my inclination to exchange thoughts and feelings, and so on. I had to give the fruit of an experience.

CARL R. ROGERS: Sounds as though you're saying that the knowledge, perhaps, or some of it, came in your twenties, but then some of the wisdom you have about interpersonal relationships came from wanting to meet people openly without wanting to dominate. And then—I see this as kind of a threefold answer—and then third, from really living the World War, but living it in your own feelings and imagination.

[1] The friend was Gustav Landauer. On Buber's relation to Landauer, see Buber, *Pointing the Way*, 'Recollection of a Death', pp. 115–120; Martin Buber, *Paths in Utopia*, trans. by R. F. C. Hull (Boston: Beacon Press, 1958), pp. 46–57 (London: Routledge, 1949); and Martin Buber, 'Landauer und die Revolution', *Masken*, Halbmonatschrift des Düsseldorfer Schauspielhauses, XIV (1918–19), No. 18/19, 282–286. Ed.

MARTIN BUBER: Just so. Because this latter was really, I cannot say it in another language, it was really a *living* with those people. People wounded, killed in the war.

CARL R. ROGERS: You felt their wounds.

MARTIN BUBER: Yes. But feeling is not sufficiently strong—the word 'feeling'.

MAURICE FRIEDMAN: Professor Roger's question reminds me of a theological student from a Baptist seminary who talked to me about Professor Buber's thought, and when he left he said, 'I must ask you a question. Professor Buber is so good. How is it he's not a Christian?'

MARTIN BUBER: Now may I tell you a story, not about me, one that is a true story, too, not just an anecdote. A Christian officer had to explain to some people in the war, in the Second War, to explain to them—soldiers—about the Jews. He began, of course, with the explanation of what Hitler means and so on, and he explained to them that the Jews are not just a barbarous race, they had a great culture, and so on; and then he addressed a Jewish soldier who was there and knew something and told him, 'Now you go on and tell them something'. And this young Jew told them something about Israel and even about Jesus. And to that, one of the soldiers answered, 'Do you mean to tell us that before your Jesus we have not been Christian people?'

CARL R. ROGERS: Well, I'd like to shift to a question that I have often wondered about. I have wondered whether your concept of what you have termed the I–Thou relationship is similar to what I see as the effective moments in a therapeutic relationship? If you would permit me, I might take a moment or two to say what I see as essential in that, and then perhaps you could comment on it from your point of view. I feel that when I'm being effective as a therapist, I enter the relationship as a subjective person, not as a scrutinizer, not as a scientist. I feel, too, that when I am most effective, then somehow I am relatively whole in that relationship, or the word that has meaning to me is 'transparent'. To be sure there may be many aspects of my life that aren't brought into the relationship, but what is brought into the relationship is transparent. There is nothing hidden. Then I think, too, that in such a relationship I feel a real willingness for this other person to *be what he is*. I call that 'acceptance'. I don't know that that's a very good word for it, but my meaning there is that I'm willing for him to possess the feelings he possesses, to hold the attitudes he holds, to be the person he is. And then another aspect of it which is important to me is that I think in those moments I am able to sense with a good deal of clarity the way his experience seems to him, really viewing it from within him, and yet without losing my own personhood or separateness in that.

Then, if in addition to those things on *my* part, my client or the person with whom I'm working is able to sense something of those attitudes in me, then it seems to me that there is a real, experiential meeting of persons, in which each of us is changed. I think sometimes that the client is changed more than I am, but I think both of us are changed in that kind of an experience. Now, I see that as having some resemblance to the sort of thing you have talked about in the I–Thou relationship. Yet I suspect there are differences. I would be interested very much in your comments on how that description seems to you in relation to what you have thought of in terms of two persons meeting in an I–Thou kind of relationship.

MARTIN BUBER: Now I may try to ask questions, too, about what you mean. First of all, I would say, this is the action of a therapist. This is a very good example for a certain moment of dialogic existence. I mean, two persons have a certain situation in common. This situation is, from your point of view—point is not a good word, but let's say from your point of view—it is a sick man coming to you and asking a particular kind of help. Now—

CARL R. ROGERS: May I interrupt there?

MARTIN BUBER: Please do.

CARL R. ROGERS: I feel that if from my point of view this is a *sick* person, then probably I'm not going to be of as much help as I might be. I feel this is a *person*. Yes, somebody else may call him sick, or if I look at him from an objective point of view, then I might agree, too, 'Yes, he's sick'. But in entering a relationship, it seems to me if I am looking upon it as 'I am a relatively well person and this is a sick person'—

MARTIN BUBER: Which I don't mean.

CARL R. ROGERS: —it's no good.

MARTIN BUBER: I don't mean it. Let me leave out this word sick. A man coming to you for help. The essential difference between your role in this situation and his is obvious. He comes for help to you. You don't come for help to him. And not only this, but you are *able*, more or less, to help him. He can do different things to you, but not help you. And not this alone. You *see* him, *really*. I don't mean that you cannot be mistaken, but you *see* him, just as you said, as he *is*. He cannot, by far, cannot *see you*. Not only in the degree, but even in the kind of seeing. You are, of course, a very important person for him. But not a person whom he wants to see and to know and is able to. He is floundering around, he comes to you. He is, may I say, entangled in your life, in your thoughts, in your being, your communication, and so on. But he is not interested in you as you. It cannot be. You are interested, you say so and you are right, in him as this person. This kind of detached presence he cannot have and give. Now this is the first point as far as I see it. And the second is—Now please, you may interrupt me any moment.

CARL R. ROGERS: I really want to understand that. The fact that I am able to see him with less distortion than he does me, and that I do have the role of helping him and that he's not trying to know me in that same sense—that's what you mean by this detached presence? I just wanted to make sure.

MARTIN BUBER: Yes, only this.

CARL R. ROGERS: O.K.

MARTIN BUBER: Now, the second fact, as far as I see, is in this *situation* that you have in common with him, but from two sides. You're on one side of the situation on the, may I say so, more or less active, and he in a more or less patient, not entirely active, not entirely passive, of course—but relatively. And this situation, let us now look on this common situation from your point of view and from his point of view. The same situation. You can see it, feel it, experience it from the two sides. From your side, seeing him, observing him, knowing him, helping him—from your side and from his side. You can experience, I would venture to say, bodily, his side of the situation. When you do, so to speak, something to him, you feel yourself touched first by what you do to him. He cannot do it at all. You are at your side and at his side at the same time. Here and there, or let's rather say, there and here. Where he is and where you are. He cannot be but where he is. And this, you will, you not only will, you want, your inner necessities may be sure as you are. I accept that. I have no objection at all. But the *situation* has an objection. You have necessarily another attitude to the situation than he has. You are able to do something that he is not able. You are not equals and cannot be. You have the great task, self-imposed—a great self-imposed task to supplement this need of his and to do rather more than in the normal situation. But, of course, there are limits, and I may be allowed to tell you certainly in your experience as a therapist, as a healing person or helping to healing, you must experience it again and again—the limits to simple humanity. To simple humanity meaning being I and my partner, so to speak, *alike* to one another, on the same plane. I see you *mean* being on the same plane, but you cannot. There is not only you, your mode of thinking, your mode of doing, there is also a certain situation—we are so and so—which may sometimes be tragic, even more terrible than what we call tragic. You *cannot* change this. Humanity, human will, human understanding, are not everything. There is some reality confronting us. We cannot forget it for a moment.

CARL R. ROGERS: Well, what you've said certainly stirs up lots of reactions in me. One of them, I think, is this. Let me begin first on a point that I think we would agree on—I suspect that you would agree that if this client comes to the point where he can experience what he is expressing, but also can experience my understanding of it and reaction to it, and so on, then really therapy is just about over.

MARTIN BUBER: Yes. But this is not what I mean.

CARL R. ROGERS: O.K. But one other thing that I feel is this. I've sometimes wondered whether this is simply a personal idiosyncracy of mine, but it seems to me that when another person is really expressing himself and his experience and so on, I don't feel, in the way that you've described, different from him. That is—I don't know quite how to put this—but I feel as though in that moment his way of looking at his experience, distorted though it might be, is something I can look upon as having equal authority, equal validity with the way I see life and experience. It seems to me *that* really is the basis of helping, in a sense.

MARTIN BUBER: Yes.

CARL R. ROGERS: And I do feel there's a real sense of equality between us.

MARTIN BUBER: No doubt of it. But I am not speaking now about your feeling but about a real situation. I mean you too look, as you just said, on *his* experience. Neither you nor he look on *your* experience. The subject is exclusively he and his experience. He cannot in the course of, let's say, a talk with you, he cannot change his position and ask you, 'Oh, Doctor, where were you yesterday? Oh, you were in the movies? What was it and how were you impressed?' He *cannot* do it. So, I see and feel very well your feeling, your attitude, your taking part. But you cannot change the given situation. There is something objectively real that confronts you. Not only he confronts you, the person, but also the situation. You cannot change it.

CARL R. ROGERS: Well now, now I'm wondering who is Martin Buber, you or me, because what I feel—

MARTIN BUBER: I'm not, so to say, 'Martin Buber' as, how do you say, with quotes.

CARL R. ROGERS: In that sense, I'm not 'Carl Rogers' either.

MARTIN BUBER: You see, I'm not a quoted man who thinks so and so and so.

CARL R. ROGERS: I know. I realize that. Aside from that facetious remark, what I wanted to say is this: That I think you're quite right, that there is an objective situation there, one that could be measured, one that is real, one that various people could agree upon if they examine the situation closely. But it has been my experience that that is reality when it is viewed from the outside, and that that really has *nothing* to do with the relationship that produces therapy. That is something immediate, equal, a meeting of two persons on an equal basis—even though, in the world of I–It, it could be seen as a very unequal relationship.

MARTIN BUBER: Now, Doctor Rogers, this is the first point where we must say to one another, 'We disagree'.

CARL R. ROGERS: O.K.

MARTIN BUBER: You see, I cannot only look on you, on your part of things, on your experience. Let's take the case where I could talk to *him*, to the patient, too. I would, of course, hear from him a very different tale about this same moment. Now, you see, I am not a therapist. I'm interested in you *and* in him. I must see the situation. I must see you and him in this dialogue bounded by tragedy. Sometimes, in many cases, a tragedy that can be overcome. Just in your method. I have no objection at all to your method, you see? There is no need to speak about it. But sometimes method is not enough. You cannot do what is necessary to do. Now, let me ask you a question that seemingly has nothing to do with this, but it's the same point. You have certainly much to do with schizophrenics. Is it so?

CARL R. ROGERS: Some.

MARTIN BUBER: You have, have you, also to do, let me say, with paranoiacs?

CARL R. ROGERS: Some.

MARTIN BUBER: Now, would you say that the situation is the same in the one case and in the other? Meaning, the situation as far as it has to do with the relationship between you and the other man. Is this relationship that you describe the same kind of relationship in the one case and in the other? This is a case, a question, which interests me very much, because I was interested very much by paranoia in my youth. I know much more about schizophrenia, but I often am very much interested, and I would like to know, have you—this would mean very much—can you meet the paranoiac just in the same kind?

CARL R. ROGERS: Let me first qualify my answer to some degree. I haven't worked in a psychiatric hospital. My dealings have been with people for the most part who are able to at least make some kind of an adjustment in the community, so that I don't see the really chronically ill people. On the other hand, we do deal with individuals who are both schizophrenic and others who are certainly paranoid. One of the things that I say very tentatively, because I realize this is opposed by a great weight of psychiatric and psychological opinion, I would say that there is no difference in the relationship that I form with a normal person, a schizophrenic, a paranoid—I don't really feel any difference. That doesn't mean, of course, that when—Well, again, it's this question of looking at it from the outside. Looking at it from the outside, one can easily discern plenty of differences. But it seems to me that if therapy is effective, there is this same kind of meeting of persons no matter what the psychiatric label. One minor point in relation to something you said that struck me. It seems to me that the moment where persons are most likely to change, or I even think of it as the moments in which people *do* change, are the moments in which perhaps the relationship is experienced the same on both sides. When you said that if you talked to my patient you would get a very different picture, I agree, that would be true in regard to a great many of the things that went on in the interview. But I should expect that in those moments when real change occurred, that it would be because there had been a real meeting of persons in which it was experienced the same from both sides.

MARTIN BUBER: Yes. This is really important. This question is particularly important to me and your answer, too. A very important point in my thinking is the problem of limits. Meaning, I do something, I try something, I will something, and I give all my thoughts in existence into this doing. And then I come at a certain moment to a wall, to a boundary, to a limit that I cannot, I *cannot* ignore. This is true, also, for what interests me more than anything: human effective dialogue. Meaning by dialogue not just a talking. Dialogue can be silence. We would perhaps, without the audience. I would recommend to do it without an audience. We could sit together, or rather walk together in silence and that could be a dialogue. But so, even in dialogue, full dialogue, there is a limit set. This is why I'm interested in paranoia. Here is a limit set for dialogue. It is sometimes very difficult to talk to a schizophrenic. In certain moments, as far as my experience with this, which is, of course, how may I say, dilettante?— I can talk to a schizophrenic as far as he is willing to let me into his particular world that is his own, and that in general he does not want to have you come in, or other people. But he lets some people in. And so he may let me in, too. But in the moment when he shuts himself, I cannot go on. And the same, only in a terrible, terrifyingly strong manner, is the case with a paranoiac. He does not open himself and does not shut himself. He *is* shut. There is something else being done to him that shuts him. And I feel this terrible fate very strongly because in the world of normal men, there are just analogous cases, when a sane man behaves, not to everyone, but behaves to some people *just so*, being *shut*, and the problem is if he can be opened, if he can open himself, and so on. And this is a problem for the human in general.

MAURICE FRIEDMAN: I'm not quite satisfied in this interchange, just before the discussion of the paranoiac and schizophrenic, as to what extent it was an issue, to what extent a different use of terms, so let me ask Doctor Rogers one step further. As I understood, what Buber said was that the relationship is an I–Thou one, but not a fully reciprocal one, in the sense that while you have the meeting, nonetheless you see from his standpoint and he cannot see from yours. And in your response to that, you pointed again and again to the meeting that takes place and even to the change that may take place on both sides. But I didn't hear you ever point to the suggestion that he does not see from your standpoint, or that it is not fully reciprocal in the sense that he also is helping you. And I wondered if this might not be perhaps just a difference if not of words, of viewpoint, where you were thinking of how you feel toward him, that he is an equal person and you respect him.

MARTIN BUBER: There remains a *decisive* difference. It's not a question of objecting to helping the other. It's one thing to help the other. He is a man wanting to help the other. And his whole attitude is this active, helping attitude. There is, I wish to say, a difference by the whole heaven, but I would rather prefer to say by the whole *hell*, a difference from your attitude. This is a man in health, A man *helped* cannot think, cannot imagine helping another. How could he?

CARL R. ROGERS: But that's where some of the difference arises. Because it seems to me again that in the most real moments of therapy I don't believe that this intention to help is any more than a substratum on my part either. Surely I wouldn't be doing this work if that wasn't part of my intention. And when I first see the client, that's what I hope I will be able to do, is to be able to help him. And yet in the interchange of the moment, I don't think my mind is filled with the thought of 'now I want to help you'. It is much more 'I want to understand you. What person are you behind that paranoid screen, or behind all these schizophrenic confusions, or behind all these masks that you wear in your real life? Who are you?' It seems to me that is a desire to meet a *person*, not 'now I want to help'. It seems to me that I've learned through my experience that when we *can* meet, then help does occur, but that's a by-product.

MAURICE FRIEDMAN: Doctor Rogers, would you not agree, though, that this is not fully reciprocal in the sense that that man does not have that attitude toward you: 'I want to understand *you*. What sort of a person are *you*?'

CARL R. ROGERS: The only modification I made of that was that perhaps in the moment where real change takes place, then I wonder if it isn't reciprocal in the sense that I am able to see this individual as he is in that moment and he really senses my understanding and acceptance of him. And that I think is what is reciprocal and is perhaps what produces change.

MARTIN BUBER: I, of course, am entirely with you as far as your experience goes. I cannot be with you as far as I have to look on the whole situation. Your experience and his. You see, you give him something in order to make him equal to you. You supplement his need in his relation to you. May I say so personally, out of a certain fullness you give him what he wants in order to be *able* to be, just for this moment, so to speak, on the same plane with you. But even that is a tangent. It is a tangent which may not last but one moment. It is not the situation as far as I see, not the situation of an hour; it is a situation of minutes. And these minutes are made possible by you. Not at all by him.

CARL R. ROGERS: That last I would thoroughly agree with, but I do sense some real disagreement there because it seems to me that what I give him is permission to *be*. Which is a little different somehow from bestowing something on him.

MARTIN BUBER: I think no human being can give more than this. Making life possible for the other, if only for a moment. I'm with you.

CARL R. ROGERS: Well, if we don't look out, we'll agree.

MARTIN BUBER: Now let's go on.

CARL R. ROGERS: I really would like to shift this to another topic because as I understand what you've written, it seems to me that I discern one other type of meeting which has a lot of significance to me in my work, that as far as I know, you haven't talked about. It seems to me that one of the most important types of meeting or relationship is the person's relationship to himself. In therapy again, which I have to draw on because that's my background of experience, there are some very vivid moments in which the individual is meeting some aspect of himself, a feeling which he has never recognized before, something of a meaning in himself that he has never known before. It could be any kind of thing. It may be his intense feeling of aloneness, or the terrible hurt he has felt, or something quite positive like his courage, and so on. But at any rate, in those moments, it seems to me that there is something that partakes of the same quality that I understand in a real meeting relationship. He is in his feeling and the feeling is in him. It is something that suffuses him. He has never experienced it before. In a very real sense, I think it could be described as a real meeting with an aspect of himself that he has never met before. Now I don't know whether that seems to you like stretching the concept you've used. I suppose I would just like to get your reaction to it. Whether to you that seems like a possible type of real relationship or a meeting? I'll push this one step further. I guess I have the feeling that it is when the person has met himself in that sense, probably in a good many different aspects, that then and perhaps only then, is he really capable of meeting another in an I–Thou relationship.

MARTIN BUBER: Now here we approach a problem of language. You call something dialogue that I cannot call so. But I can explain why I cannot call it so, why I would want another term between dialogue and monologue for this. Now for what I call dialogue, there is essentially necessary the moment of surprise. I mean—

CARL R. ROGERS: You say 'surprise'?

MARTIN BUBER: Yes, being surprised. A dialogue—let's take a rather trivial image. The dialogue is like a game of chess. The whole charm of chess is that I do not know and cannot know what my partner will do. I am surprised by what he does and on this surprise the whole play is based. Now you hint at this, that a man can surprise himself. But in a very different manner from how a person can surprise another person. . . .

(*While the tape was being changed, Dr Buber went on with his description of the characteristics of a true dialogue. A second feature is that in true meeting, or dialogue, that which is different in the other person, his otherness, is prized.*)

CARL R. ROGERS: I hope that perhaps sometime I can play recordings of interviews for you to indicate how the surprise element can be there. That is, a person can be expressing something and then suddenly be hit by the meaning of that which has come from someplace in himself which he doesn't recognize. He really is *surprised* by himself. That can definitely happen. But the element that I see as being most foreign to your concept of dialogue is that it is quite true that this otherness in himself is not something to be prized. I think that in the kind of dialogue I'm talking about, within the person, that it is that otherness which probably would be broken down. And I do realize that in part the whole discussion of this may be based on a different use of words, too.

MARTIN BUBER: And you see, may I add a technical matter? I have learned in the course of my life to appreciate terms. And I think that in modern psychology, this does not exist in a sufficient measure. When I find something that is essentially different from another thing, I want a new term. I want a new concept. You see, for instance, modern psychology in general says about the unconscious that it is a certain mode of the psyche. It has no sense at all for me. If two things are so different from one another as this strain of the soul, changing in every moment, where I cannot grasp anything when I try to grasp its way from one side—this *being* in pure time, and over against this what we call the unconscious, which is not a phenomenon at all, which we have no access to at all, but have only to deal with its effects—we cannot say the first is psychic and the second is psychic, that the unconscious is something in which the psychical and the physiological are mixed; it's not enough. They penetrate one another in such a manner that in relation to the unconscious the terms 'body' and 'soul' are, so to speak, late terms, late concepts—and concepts are never reality. Now, how can we comprehend this one concept?

CARL R. ROGERS: I agree with you very much on that. I think when an experience is definitely of a different sort, then it does deserve a different term. I think we agree on that. I'd like to raise one other question that has a great deal of meaning to me, and I don't know how to put it. Let me express it something like this. As I see people coming together in relationships in therapy, I think that one of the things I have come to believe and feel and experience is that what I think of as human nature or basic human nature—that's a poor term and you may have a better way of putting it—is something that is really to be *trusted*. And it seems to me in some of your writings

I catch something of that same feeling. At any rate, it's been very much my experience in therapy that one does not need to supply motivation toward the positive or toward the constructive. That exists in the individual. In other words, if we can release what is most basic in the individual, that it will be constructive. . . .

I'll try to put it in another way. It seems to me that orthodox psychoanalysis at least has held that when the individual is revealed, when you really get down to what is within the person, he consists mostly of instincts and attitudes and so on which must be *controlled*. That runs diametrically contrary to my own experience, which is that when you get to what is deepest in the individual, that is the very aspect that can most be trusted to be constructive or to tend toward socialization or toward the development of better interpersonal relationships. Does that have meaning for you?

MARTIN BUBER: I see. I would put it in a somewhat different manner. As far as I see, when I have to do with, now let me say a problematic person, or just a sick person, a problematic person, a person that people call, or want to call, a bad person. You see, in general, the man who has really to do with what we call the spirit is called not to the good people, but just to the bad people, to the problematic, to the un- acceptable, and so on. The good people, they can be friends with them, but they don't need them. So I'm interested just in the so-called bad, problematic, and so on. And my experience is (and this is near to what you say, but somewhat different) if I come near to the reality of this person, I experience it as a *polar* reality. You see, in general we say this is either *A* or *Non-A*. It cannot be *A* and *Non-A* at the same time. It can't. I mean what you say may be trusted; I would say this stands in polar relation to what can be least trusted in this man. You cannot say, and perhaps I differ from you in this point, you cannot say, 'Oh, I detect in him just what can be trusted'. I would say now when I see him, when I grasp him more broadly and more deeply than before, I see his whole polarity and then I see how the worst in him and the best in him are dependent on one another, attached to one another. And I can help, I may be able to help him just by helping him to change the relation between the poles. Not just by choice, but by a certain strength that he gives to the one pole in relation to the other. The poles being qualitatively very alike to one another. I would say there is not as we generally think in the soul of a man good and evil opposed. There is again and again in different manners a polarity, and the poles are not good and evil, but rather yes and no, rather acceptance and refusal. And we can strengthen, or we can help him strengthen, the one positive pole. And perhaps we can even strengthen the force of direction in him because this polarity is very often directionless. It is a chaotic state. We could bring a cosmic note into it. We can help put order, put a shape into this. Because I think the good, what we may call the good, is always only direction. Not a substance.

CARL R. ROGERS: And if I get the last portion of that particularly, you're saying that perhaps we can help the individual to strengthen the yes, that is to affirm life rather than to refuse it.

MARTIN BUBER: I differ only in this word, I would not say life. I would not put an object to it.

MAURICE FRIEDMAN: My function as moderator is to sharpen issues and I feel that there are two interrelated things that have been touched on here, but maybe not brought out. When Doctor Rogers first asked Professor Buber about his attitude toward psychotherapy, he mentioned as one of the factors which entered into his approach to therapy, acceptance. Now, Professor Buber often uses the term 'confirmation', and it is my own feeling both from what they said tonight and my knowledge of their writings, that it might be of real importance to clarify whether both men mean somewhat the same. In addition to saying that acceptance is a warm regard for the other and a respect for his individuality, for him as a person of unconditional worth, Doctor Rogers writes that it means 'an acceptance of and regard for his attitudes of the moment, no matter how much they may contradict other attitudes he has held in the past. And this acceptance of each fluctuating aspect of this other person makes it for him a relationship of warmth and safety'.[1] Now, I wonder whether Professor Buber would look on confirmation as similar to that, or would he see confirmation as including, perhaps, *not* being accepted, including some demand on the other that might mean in a sense a nonacceptance of his feelings at the moment in order to confirm him later.

MARTIN BUBER: I would say every true existential relationship between two persons begins with acceptance. By acceptance I mean being able to tell, or rather not to tell, but only to make it felt to the other person, that I accept him just as he is. I take you just as you are.

[1] I was quoting an essay, 'Some Hypotheses Regarding the Facilitation of Personal Growth', later published in Carl R. Rogers, *On Becoming a Person* (Boston: Houghton Mifflin Co., 1961), p. 34 (London: Constable, 1961). Ed.

Well, so, but it is not yet what I mean by confirming the other. Because accepting, this is just accepting how he ever is in this moment, in this actuality of his. Confirming means first of all, accepting the whole potentiality of the other and making even a decisive difference in his potentiality, and of course we can be mistaken again and again in this, but it's just a chance between human beings. I can recognize in him, know in him, more or less, the person he has been (I can say it only in this word) *created* to become. In the simple factual language, we do not find the term for it because we don't find in it the term, the concept *being meant to become*. This is what we must, as far as we can, grasp, if not in the first moment, then after this. And now I not only accept the other as he is, but I confirm him, in myself, and then in him, in relation to this potentiality that is meant by him and it can now be developed, it can evolve, it can answer the reality of life. He can do more or less to this scope but I can, too, do something. And this is with goals even deeper than acceptance. Let's take, for example, man and a woman, man and wife. He says, not expressly, but just by his whole relation to her, 'I accept you as you are'. But this does *not* mean, 'I don't want you to change'. Rather it says, 'Just by my accepting love, I discover in you what you are meant to become'. This is, of course, not anything to be expressed in massive terms. But it may be that it grows and grows with the years of common life. This is what you mean?

CARL R. ROGERS: Yes. And I think that sounds very much like this quality that is in the experience that I think of as acceptance, though I have tended to put it differently. I think that we do accept the individual *and* his potentiality. I think it's a real question whether we could accept the individual as he is, because often he is in pretty sad shape, if it were not for the fact that we also in some sense realize and recognize his potentiality. I guess I feel, too, that acceptance of the most complete sort, acceptance of this person as he is, is the strongest factor making for change that I know. In other words, I think that does release change or release potentiality to find that as I am, I am fully accepted—then I can't help but change. Because then I feel there is no longer any need for defensive barriers, so then what takes over are the forward moving processes of life itself, I think.

MARTIN BUBER: I'm afraid I'm not so sure of that as you are, perhaps because I'm not a therapist. And I have necessarily to do with that problematic type. In my relationship to him I cannot do without this polarity. I cannot put this aside. As I said, I have to do with both men. I have to do with the problematic in him. And there are cases when I must help him against himself. He wants my help against himself. You see, the first thing of all is that he trusts me. Yes, life has become baseless for him. He cannot tread on firm soil, on firm earth. He is, so to speak, suspended in the air. And what does he want? What he wants is a being not only whom he can trust as a man trusts another, but a being that gives him now the certitude that 'there *is* a soil, there *is* an existence. The world is not condemned to deprivation, degeneration, destruction. The world *can* be redeemed. *I* can be redeemed because there is this trust.' And if this is reached, now I can help this man even in his struggle against himself. And this I can do only if I distinguish between accepting and confirming.

MAURICE FRIEDMAN: May I ask one last question? My impression is that, on the one hand, there has been more insistence by Doctor Rogers on the fuller reciprocity of the I–Thou relation in therapy and less by Doctor Buber, but on the other, I get the impression that Doctor Rogers is more client-centred, more concerned with the becoming of the person. He speaks too in a recent article[1] of being able to trust one's organism to find satisfaction, to express oneself. And he speaks of the locus of value as being inside one, whereas I get the impression from my encounter with Doctor Buber that he sees value as more in 'the between'. I wonder, is this a real issue between the two of you?

CARL R. ROGERS: I might give an expression of my view on that. It puts it in quite different terms than those you've used, but I think it is related to the same thing. As I've tried to think about it in recent months, it seems to me that you could speak of the goal toward which therapy moves, and I guess the goal toward which maturity moves in an individual, as being *becoming*, or being knowingly and acceptingly that which one most deeply is. That, too, expresses a real trust in the process which we are, that may not entirely be shared between us tonight.

MARTIN BUBER: Perhaps it would be of a certain aid if I ask a problem that I found when reading this article of yours,[1] or a problem that approached me. You speak about persons, and the concept 'persons' is seemingly very near to the concept 'individual'. I would think that

---

[1] Both Martin Buber and I were referring to 'What It Means to Become a Person', which is now Chapter 6 of Rogers, *On Becoming a Person*. Ed.

it is advisable to distinguish between them. An individual is just a certain uniqueness of a human being. And it can develop just by developing with uniqueness. This is what Jung calls individuation. He may become more and more an individual without becoming more and more human. I know many examples of man having become very, very individual, very distinct from others, very developed in their such-and-suchness without being at all what I would like to call a man. The individual is just this uniqueness; being able to be developed thus and thus. But a person, I would say, is an individual living really with the world. And *with* the world, I don't mean *in* the world—just in *real contact*, in real reciprocity with the world in all the points in which the world can meet man. I don't say only with man, because sometimes we meet the world in other shapes than in that of man. But this is what I would call a person and if I may say expressly Yes and No to certain phenomena, I'm *against* individuals and *for* persons.

MAURICE FRIEDMAN: We are deeply indebted to Doctor Rogers and Doctor Buber for a unique dialogue. It is certainly unique in my experience: it is a *real* dialogue, taking place in front of an audience, and I think that it is in part because of what they were willing to give us and did give us; and part was because you [the audience] took part in a sort of trialogue, or adding me, a quatralogue in which you silently participated.[1]

[1] A significant confirmation of my own feeling about this dialogue is the fact that, as a result of it, Martin Buber made me cancel the last paragraph in the manuscript of 'Elements of the Interhuman' (Chapter III of this book) in which he had stated that it was impossible to have a dialogue in front of a public. The deleted paragraph read: 'In our time when the understanding of the essence of genuine dialogue has become so rare, its presuppositions are so fundamentally misunderstood by the false sense of public life that it is imagined that such a dialogue can be carried on before a public of interested listeners, with the help of the appropriate publicity. But a public debate, no matter how "high level", cannot be spontaneous, or immediate, or unreserved; a radio discussion put on to be listened to is separated by a chasm from genuine dialogue.' Ed.

INDEX

(Prepared by Maurice Friedman, Editor)

[1] Where the author's name is not given, the book or essay is by Martin Buber.
Ed.

INDEX